The Type 2 Diabetes Crockpot Cookbook

100 Complete Healthy Slow Cooking Recipes for Everyday Life

Etta William

FOR MORE INTERSTING BOOKS FROM THE AUTHOR KINDLY SCAN THE BARCODE BELOW

OR CLICK ON HERE

About author

Etta William is a multi-talented British American author, nutritionist, and writer, known for her expertise in the fields of health, nutrition, diet, and cookbooks. Etta's journey in the world of nutrition and culinary arts began with her academic pursuits at the prestigious Massachusetts Institute of Technology (MIT), where she honed her knowledge and skills in various aspects of nutrition and healthy living.

As a seasoned nutritionist, Etta has dedicated her career to helping individuals make informed choices about their diets and overall well-being. Her passion for promoting healthy eating and lifestyles shines through in her work, where she combines scientific knowledge with a practical approach to guide readers and enthusiasts on their paths to better health.

Etta's commitment to her craft extends beyond her profession as a nutritionist. She has established herself as a prolific writer, with a particular focus on health, nutrition, and cookbooks. Her writing is not only informative but also highly accessible, making complex dietary concepts and recipes easily understandable to a broad audience.

Through her books, Etta shares her insights and recipes, aiming to inspire and empower readers to embrace a healthier way of life. Her cookbooks are a testament to her culinary prowess and her dedication to creating dishes that are both delicious and nutritious, providing readers with a wealth of options to nourish their bodies.

With a unique blend of scientific knowledge and a passion for good food, Etta William continues to make a significant impact in the world of health and nutrition. Her work serves as a valuable resource for those seeking to improve their dietary choices and embark on a journey towards better health and well-being. Etta's contributions as an author and nutritionist have undoubtedly enriched the lives of many, offering guidance and inspiration on the path to a healthier lifestyle.

Table Of Content

Introduction

Understanding Type 2 Diabetes and the Role of Crockpot Cooking's

A chronic illness that affects millions of people worldwide is type 2 diabetes. The hallmark of this metabolic disorder is elevated blood glucose levels, which result from the body's failure to appropriately control blood sugar levels. Anyone who has Type 2 diabetes or provides care for someone who does must have a thorough understanding of the disease, its effects, and how important diet is to be managing it.

Understanding Type 2 Diabetes

Adult-onset diabetes, also known as type 2 diabetes, is a complicated medical condition that affects how well the body uses insulin. The pancreas secretes the hormone insulin, which is essential for controlling blood sugar levels. People with Type 2 diabetes are unable to maintain normal blood sugar levels because their cells become resistant to the effects of insulin. This causes a condition known as hyperglycemia, or elevated blood glucose, which can cause several health issues if left unchecked.

The gradual onset of Type 2 diabetes is one of its distinguishing characteristics. In contrast to Type 1 diabetes, which usually manifests as a lack of insulin production in childhood, Type 2 diabetes is more likely to develop gradually and is strongly associated with genetics and lifestyle choices. Obesity, inactivity, and an unhealthful diet are risk factors. Type 2 diabetes can occur more frequently due to genetic predisposition, but lifestyle choices have a significant influence as well.

Since Type 2 diabetes is primarily a preventable and manageable condition, it is crucial to understand it. Blood sugar control can be achieved through lifestyle modifications, especially dietary changes, although some people may need to take medication or receive insulin therapy. Those who have Type 2 diabetes can greatly improve their health and quality of life by making educated food choices.

The Role of Diet in Managing Type 2 Diabetes:

The key to controlling Type 2 diabetes is diet. Blood sugar levels in people with this illness can be directly and quickly affected by what they eat. Making the correct dietary decisions can improve general health and well-being, lower the risk of complications, and help stabilize blood sugar.

Keeping blood sugar levels constant throughout the day is one of the main objectives of dietary management for people with Type 2 diabetes. This entails controlling the consumption of carbohydrates, which have the biggest impact on blood sugar. During digestion, glucose from carbohydrates is produced, which raises blood sugar levels. To control blood sugar, one must limit one's intake of carbohydrates, which are commonly measured in grams.

An important component of diet-based Type 2 diabetes management is emphasizing balanced nutrition. This entails eating a range of foods that are high in fiber, vitamins, minerals, and lean protein, among other important nutrients. Macronutrient balance—that is, the proper ratio of fat, protein, and carbohydrates—is essential for good general health and sugar regulation.

Furthermore, one of the most important aspects of diet management is keeping an eye on portion sizes. Blood sugar levels can spike as a result of overindulging, while hypoglycemia (low blood sugar) is the result of undereating. For people with Type 2 diabetes, striking the correct balance is crucial, and it's a skill that can be developed with practice and experience.

A common dietary strategy for Type 2 diabetes is to select low-glycemic index (GI) foods. Foods containing carbohydrates are ranked on the GI scale according to how quickly their blood sugar levels rise. Low GI foods digest more slowly, which causes blood sugar to rise gradually but steadily. This aids people in avoiding the sharp rises and falls in blood sugar that are linked to high-GI foods.

It is impossible to exaggerate the role that diet plays in managing Type 2 diabetes. It gives people the ability to take charge of their health and wellbeing. Food choices continue to be a basic and easily accessible tool in the management of diabetes, even though medication and insulin therapy may be necessary in certain situations.

Benefits of Crockpot Cooking for Type 2 Diabetes:

Slow cooking, or crockpot cooking, has become more and more well-liked as a useful and convenient way to make meals in recent years. However, what makes it especially beneficial for those who have Type 2 diabetes?

Slow Cooking for Controlled Blood Sugar Levels:
Slow cooking is cooking food in a crockpot or slow cooker at low temperatures for several hours, usually. Compared to other cooking methods, this one can help regulate blood sugar levels more effectively, which makes it beneficial for people with Type 2 diabetes.

The flavors of the ingredients can blend during the slow, gradual cooking process, resulting in a tasty and filling dish. The slow and steady pace of cooking can help with blood sugar regulation. It stops quick spikes in blood sugar that can happen when cooking quickly and at a high temperature. Crockpot meals typically affect blood sugar levels more gently, assisting in the maintenance of steady levels throughout the day.

Furthermore, lean meat cuts, an abundance of vegetables, and whole grains are frequently used in slow cooking—all of which are advantageous for people with Type 2 diabetes. These components help to provide a balanced diet, which makes crockpot meals a wise choice for health-conscious people.

Portion Control and Nutritional Balance:
A key component of managing Type 2 diabetes is portion control, which slow cooking can help with in a number of ways. Because crockpots are available in multiple sizes, one can precisely regulate how much food is prepared. This implies that people can prepare meals in serving sizes that correspond to their dietary requirements and preferences.

Apart from promoting portion control, slow cooking inherently promotes well-balanced and nourishing meals. Complex carbohydrates, lean proteins, and a range of vegetables are frequently found in recipes. These components support the upkeep of a balanced, diabetes-friendly diet. In addition to maintaining the nutritional value of ingredients, slow cooking techniques guarantee that the vitamins and minerals in the finished dish are retained.

Making Diabetes-Friendly Meals Convenient:

Finding quick and easy ways to prepare nutritious meals is one of the biggest problems facing people with Type 2 diabetes. This problem is solved by the slow cooker, which provides an easy and quick cooking option.

Cooking in a crockpot is meant to be simple. People can just put their ingredients in the slow cooker and let it take care of the rest, as it requires very little active preparation on their part. For people with hectic schedules who might find it difficult to find the time and energy to prepare elaborate meals, this convenience is extremely helpful.

One more big benefit of crockpot cooking is its versatility. With this method, people can cook a variety of foods, including breakfast, dinner, and even desserts. This variety makes it possible to have satisfying and pleasurable meals that are also diabetes-friendly, which lessens the temptation to choose less healthful options.

In conclusion, there are numerous advantages to using a crockpot for managing Type 2 diabetes. Controlled, slow cooking facilitates stable blood sugar levels and makes achieving nutritional balance and portion control simple. Slow cooking is an accessible and useful option for people who want to control their diabetes with food because of its ease of use. With these benefits, those with Type 2 diabetes may find that crockpot cooking is an effective tool for improving their health and blood sugar management.

Benefits of the Book:

For people with Type 2 diabetes and their families, "The Type 2 Diabetes Crockpot Cookbook" provides many helpful advantages. These include:

Focused on Diabetes-Friendly Recipes:
This cookbook has been carefully chosen to offer a variety of recipes that are suitable for people with diabetes. Every recipe has been carefully designed to accommodate the dietary requirements and preferences of people who have Type 2 diabetes. The book makes sure that people with diabetes can

enjoy tasty and fulfilling meals without sacrificing their health by concentrating on recipes that are suitable for people with this condition.

Nutritional Information Provided for Each Recipe:
The nutritional data included with each recipe in this book is one of its best features. Every recipe has a comprehensive nutritional analysis that includes calorie counts, protein, fat, carbs, and fiber content. Because of this openness, readers are better equipped to control their blood sugar levels by making educated dietary decisions.

With this information easily accessible, people with Type 2 diabetes can easily include these recipes in their meal plans, understanding exactly how each dish contributes to their daily dietary objectives.

Suitable for Individuals and Families Managing Type 2 Diabetes:
The cookbook's adaptability goes beyond personal meal planning. It is intended to meet the requirements of families as well as individuals managing Type 2 diabetes. Meals for one, two, or more people can be prepared with ease thanks to the recipes' adjustable serving sizes.

The book also recognizes the significance of cooking for the family. Whether or not a person has diabetes, it provides options that everyone at the table can enjoy. For families with children who have Type 2 diabetes, this inclusivity makes mealtimes more pleasurable by fostering a sense of community and doing away with the need for separate meals.

Tips and Guidelines for Cooking with Type 2 Diabetes:

Alongside a plethora of diabetes-friendly recipes, the book offers a helpful set of pointers and instructions for cooking when you have Type 2 diabetes:

Choosing Diabetes-Friendly Ingredients:
The cookbook provides advice on how to choose the best ingredients for dishes that are diabetes-friendly. It emphasizes how crucial it is to choose whole grains, lean proteins, low-GI foods, and an abundance of vegetables. Readers can confidently choose ingredients that support stable blood sugar levels by knowing how to make informed decisions at the grocery store.

Monitoring Carbohydrate and Sugar Intake:

The consumption of sugar and carbohydrates is crucial for people with Type 2 diabetes. The book provides helpful guidance on how to keep an eye on these diet-related aspects. It informs readers on how to estimate and control their daily intake of carbohydrates to prevent blood sugar surges. People with diabetes can better manage their condition by tracking their sugar and carbohydrate intake and making thoughtful food choices.

Balancing Meals for Better Blood Sugar Control:

Meals that are well-balanced are essential to managing diabetes. The cookbook offers guidance on how to prepare meals that are balanced and encourage stable blood sugar levels. It advises readers to make sure they get the proper proportion of healthy fats, proteins, and carbs at each meal by incorporating a range of food groups.

The significance of portion control is also emphasized in the book, since eating too much food can cause blood sugar swings. People with Type 2 diabetes can improve their blood sugar control and general health by planning their meals with portion control and balance.

In summary, "The Type 2 Diabetes Crockpot Cookbook" provides a wide range of advantages, including diabetic-friendly recipes, dietary guidance, and applicability for both individuals and families with Type 2 diabetes. Additionally, it offers crucial pointers and recommendations for improving blood sugar regulation and making educated food decisions. For individuals who are trying to live a healthier and more diabetes-aware lifestyle, this cookbook is an invaluable tool.

Diabetes-Friendly Breakfast Recipes

1. Overnight Oatmeal with Berries

Ingredients:

- 1/2 cup old-fashioned oats

- 1 cup unsweetened almond milk

- 1/4 cup fresh mixed berries (strawberries, blueberries, raspberries)

- 1 tablespoon chia seeds

- 1/2 teaspoon vanilla extract

- 1/4 teaspoon cinnamon

- 1 teaspoon honey (optional for sweetness)

Procedure:

1. Combine the oats, almond milk, chia seeds, cinnamon, vanilla extract, and mason jar or other container.

2. Blend thoroughly and cover the jar. Keep cold all night.

3. Add some fresh mixed berries to the oatmeal in the morning, and if you'd like, drizzle some honey on top.

4. Savor your delicious and nutritious oatmeal for breakfast!

Time Frame:

- Preparation Time: 5 minutes

- Total Time: Overnight (Preparation is done the night before)

Yield:

- 1 serving

Nutritional Value:

- Calories: 300

- Carbohydrates: 45g

- Protein: 7g

- Fat: 10g

- Fiber: 9g

- Sugar: 9g

2. Veggie and Cheese Omelette

Ingredients:

- 2 large eggs

- 1/4 cup diced bell peppers (red, green, or yellow)

- 1/4 cup diced onions

- 1/4 cup diced tomatoes

- 2 tablespoons shredded low-fat cheese

- Salt and pepper to taste

- Cooking spray or olive oil for greasing the pan

Procedure:

1. Beat the eggs and add salt and pepper to taste in a bowl.

2. Grease a non-stick skillet with cooking spray or olive oil and heat it over medium heat.

3. To the pan, add the diced tomatoes, onions, and bell peppers. Let them cook for a few minutes until they soften.

4. Over the sautéed vegetables, pour the beaten eggs and cook until the edges set.

5. Top half of the omelette with shredded cheese.

6. Gently fold the remaining omelette half over the cheese.

7. Cook for one or two minutes, or until the omelette is thoroughly cooked and the cheese melts.

8. Transfer the omelette to a plate and enjoy it warm.

Time Frame:

- Preparation Time: 10 minutes

- Total Time: 15 minutes

Yield:

- 1 serving

Nutritional Value:

- Calories: 220

- Carbohydrates: 8g

- Protein: 18g

- Fat: 13g

- Fiber: 2g

- Sugar: 4g

3. Cinnamon Apple Porridge

Ingredients:

- 1/2 cup old-fashioned oats

- 1 cup water

- 1/2 apple, peeled, cored, and diced

- 1/2 teaspoon ground cinnamon

- 1 teaspoon honey (optional for sweetness)

Procedure:

1. Add the oats and water to a saucepan. After bringing to a boil, lower the heat to a simmer.

2. To the saucepan, add the diced apple and ground cinnamon. Mix thoroughly.

3. Cook, stirring occasionally, until the apple is soft and the oats are creamy, about 5 to 7 minutes.

4. Drizzle with honey for sweetness, if desired.

5. Enjoy the warming tastes of apple and cinnamon with the porridge served in a bowl.

Time Frame:

- Preparation Time: 5 minutes

- Baking Time: 5-7 minutes

- Total Time: 10-12 minutes

Yield:

- 1 serving

Nutritional Value:

- Calories: 250

- Carbohydrates: 48g

- Protein: 6g

- Fat: 4g

- Fiber: 6g

- Sugar: 11g

4. Greek Yogurt Parfait

Ingredients:

- 1/2 cup plain Greek yogurt

- 1/4 cup fresh mixed berries (strawberries, blueberries, raspberries)

- 1 tablespoon honey or agave nectar (optional for sweetness)

- 2 tablespoons granola

- 1/2 teaspoon vanilla extract

Procedure:

1. Start with a layer of Greek yogurt in a glass or bowl.

2. Top the yogurt with a layer of fresh mixed berries.

3. If desired, drizzle with agave nectar or honey.

4. To give the berries more taste and texture, scatter granola on top.

5. As desired, repeat the layering.

6. For added flavor, add a dash of vanilla extract at the end.

7. Savor this delicious parfait made with Greek yogurt.

Time Frame:

- Preparation Time: 5 minutes

- Total Time: 5 minutes

Yield:

- 1 serving

Nutritional Value:

- Calories: 320

- Carbohydrates: 50g

- Protein: 15g

- Fat: 8g

- Fiber: 5g

- Sugar: 28g

5. Scrambled Eggs with Spinach and Tomatoes

Ingredients:

- 2 large eggs

- 1 cup fresh spinach leaves

- 1/2 cup diced tomatoes

- Salt and pepper to taste

- Cooking spray or olive oil for greasing the pan

Procedure:

1. Beat the eggs and add salt and pepper to taste in a bowl.

2. Grease a non-stick skillet with cooking spray or olive oil and heat it over medium heat.

3. Toss in the diced tomatoes and fresh spinach leaves. Sauté the tomatoes until they are soft and the spinach has wilted.

4. Over the sautéed spinach and tomatoes, pour the beaten eggs. As they cook, gently stir them.

5. Cook the eggs until they are completely set but not overly dry.

6. Spoon the scrambled eggs onto a plate along with the tomatoes and spinach.

7. Serve hot and savor a protein-rich, healthful breakfast.

Time Frame:

- Preparation Time: 5 minutes

- Total Time: 10 minutes

Yield:

- 1 serving

Nutritional Value:

- Calories: 220

- Carbohydrates: 8g

- Protein: 16g

- Fat: 15g

- Fiber: 2g

- Sugar: 3g

6. Quinoa Breakfast Bowl

Ingredients:

- 1/2 cup cooked quinoa

- 1/4 cup plain Greek yogurt

- 1/4 cup fresh mixed berries (strawberries, blueberries, raspberries)

- 1 tablespoon chopped nuts (e.g., almonds, walnuts)

- 1 teaspoon honey or maple syrup (optional for sweetness)

- 1/2 teaspoon cinnamon

- 1/2 teaspoon vanilla extract

Procedure:

1. Start with a bed of cooked quinoa in a bowl.

2. Top with a layer of plain Greek yogurt.

3. For extra taste and texture, sprinkle chopped nuts and fresh mixed berries on top.

4. Drizzle with maple syrup or honey for sweetness, if preferred.

5. For added flavor, add a dash of vanilla extract and sprinkle with cinnamon.

6. Combine the ingredients and savor your nourishing breakfast bowl of quinoa.

Time Frame:

- Preparation Time: 5 minutes

- Total Time: 5 minutes

Yield:

- 1 serving

Nutritional Value:

- Calories: 280

- Carbohydrates: 35g

- Protein: 11g

- Fat: 9g

- Fiber: 6g

- Sugar: 9g

7. Breakfast Burrito with Whole Wheat Tortilla

Ingredients:

- 1 whole wheat tortilla

- 2 large eggs, scrambled

- 1/4 cup diced bell peppers (red, green, or yellow)

- 1/4 cup diced onions

- 1/4 cup black beans, drained and rinsed

- 2 tablespoons shredded low-fat cheese

- Salsa for topping (optional)

- Salt and pepper to taste

- Cooking spray or olive oil for greasing the pan

Procedure:

1. The whole wheat tortilla should be warmed and slightly crispy after one minute on each side in a nonstick skillet.

2. Add the chopped onions and bell peppers to the same skillet. Cook them until they are soft.

3. To the skillet, add the black beans and scrambled eggs. Cook the eggs until they are set through.

4. Over the egg mixture, scatter the cheese shreds.

5. Spoon the blend onto the heated tortilla.

6. To create a burrito, roll up the tortilla.

7. Serve hot, with salsa on top if you'd like.

Time Frame:

- Preparation Time: 5 minutes

- Total Time: 10 minutes

Yield:

- 1 serving

Nutritional Value:

- Calories: 350

- Carbohydrates: 40g

- Protein: 21g

- Fat: 12g

- Fiber: 8g

- Sugar: 3g

8. Chia Seed Pudding

Ingredients:

- 2 tablespoons chia seeds

- 1/2 cup unsweetened almond milk

- 1/4 teaspoon vanilla extract

- 1/2 cup diced fresh fruit (e.g., mango, kiwi, or your choice)

- 1 teaspoon honey (optional for sweetness)

Procedure:

1. Mix the unsweetened almond milk, vanilla extract, and chia seeds in a bowl.

2. After giving the mixture a good stir, chill it for several hours or overnight to allow it to thicken.

3. Stir the chia pudding and sprinkle fresh fruit dice on top in the morning.

4. Drizzle with honey for sweetness, if desired.

5. Savor a filling and healthy chia seed pudding.

Time Frame:

- Preparation Time: 5 minutes

- Total Time: 4 hours or overnight (for chia pudding to thicken)

Yield:

- 1 serving

Nutritional Value:

- Calories: 280

- Carbohydrates: 35g

- Protein: 6g

- Fat: 12g

- Fiber: 10g

- Sugar: 16g

9. Breakfast Frittata with Turkey Sausage

Ingredients:

- 2 large eggs

- 1/4 cup cooked and crumbled turkey sausage

- 1/4 cup diced bell peppers (red, green, or yellow)

- 1/4 cup diced onions

- Salt and pepper to taste

- Cooking spray or olive oil for greasing the pan

Procedure:

1. Beat the eggs and add salt and pepper to taste in a bowl.

2. Grease a non-stick skillet with cooking spray or olive oil and heat it over medium heat.

3. To the pan, add the chopped onions and bell peppers. Let them cook for a few minutes until they soften.

4. Over the sautéed vegetables, scatter the crumbled turkey sausage.

5. Over the mixture in the skillet, pour the beaten eggs, and cook until the edges firm.

6. Allow the frittata to cook for a minute or two, or until the bottom is lightly golden and the eggs are set.

7. Transfer the frittata to a plate and enjoy it warm.

Time Frame:

- Preparation Time: 10 minutes

- Total Time: 15 minutes

Yield:

- 1 serving

Nutritional Value:

- Calories: 290

- Carbohydrates: 7g

- Protein: 20g

- Fat: 19g

- Fiber: 2g

- Sugar: 2g

10. Baked Avocado and Egg

Ingredients:

- 1 ripe avocado, halved and pitted

- 2 large eggs

- Salt and pepper to taste

- Fresh herbs for garnish (e.g., parsley or chives)

- Hot sauce or salsa (optional)

Procedure:

1. Turn the oven on to 375°F, or 190°C.

2. To make a larger well, scoop out a small portion of the avocado flesh from each half.

3. To keep the avocado halves stable, place them in a baking dish.

4. In each half of an avocado, crack an egg. Add pepper and salt for seasoning.

5. Bake for 12 to 15 minutes, or until the eggs are cooked to your preferred consistency, in a preheated oven.

6. Serve hot, garnished with fresh herbs. If you would like more flavor, you can add salsa or hot sauce.

Time Frame:

- Preparation Time: 5 minutes

- Baking Time: 12-15 minutes

- Total Time: 17-20 minutes

Yield:

- 1 serving

Nutritional Value:

- Calories: 320

- Carbohydrates: 12g

- Protein: 12g

- Fat: 28g

- Fiber: 9g

- Sugar: 2g

Low-Carb Lunch And Dinner Recipes

1. Chicken and Vegetable Stir-Fry

Ingredients:

- 4 oz boneless, skinless chicken breast, sliced into strips

- 1 cup mixed vegetables (broccoli, bell peppers, snap peas)

- 1 clove garlic, minced

- 1 tablespoon low-sodium soy sauce

- 1/2 tablespoon olive oil

- Salt and pepper to taste

Procedure:

1. In a nonstick skillet set over medium-high heat, warm the olive oil.

2. When the chicken strips are no longer pink, add them and cook.

3. To the skillet, add the mixed vegetables and minced garlic. The vegetables should be stir-fried for a few minutes to make them crisp-tender.

4. Add a drizzle of low-sodium soy sauce and mix thoroughly.

5. To taste, add salt and pepper for seasoning.

6. Serve hot stir-fried chicken and vegetables and savor your low-carb dinner.

Time Frame:

- Preparation Time: 10 minutes

- Cooking Time: 10 minutes

- Total Time: 20 minutes

Yield:

- 1 serving

Nutritional Value:

- Calories: 280

- Carbohydrates: 12g

- Protein: 30g

- Fat: 10g

- Fiber: 4g

- Sugar: 4g

2. Turkey and Spinach Stuffed Peppers

Ingredients:

- 2 large bell peppers, any color

- 4 oz lean ground turkey

- 1 cup fresh spinach, chopped

- 1/4 cup diced tomatoes (canned or fresh)

- 1/4 cup shredded low-fat cheese

- 1/2 teaspoon Italian seasoning

- Salt and pepper to taste

Procedure:

1. Turn the oven on to 375°F, or 190°C.

2. Slice off the bell peppers' tops, then take out the seeds and membranes.

3. Brown the ground turkey over medium heat in a skillet. Add salt, pepper, and Italian seasoning to taste.

4. To the skillet, add the diced tomatoes and chopped spinach. Cook until the mixture is well combined and the spinach has wilted.

5. Stuff the turkey and spinach mixture into the bell peppers.

6. After placing the filled peppers in a baking dish, cover it with foil.

7. Bake the peppers for 25 to 30 minutes, or until they are soft.

8. Take off the foil, cover with the shredded cheese, and bake for a further five to seven minutes, or until the cheese is melted and beginning to turn golden.

9. Enjoy your low-carb stuffed peppers while they're hot.

Time Frame:

- Preparation Time: 20 minutes

- Baking Time: 30-37 minutes

- Total Time: 50-57 minutes

Yield:

- 2 servings (1 stuffed pepper per serving)

Nutritional Value:

- Calories (per serving): 220

- Carbohydrates: 14g

- Protein: 22g

- Fat: 8g

- Fiber: 5g

- Sugar: 6g

3. Lemon Herb Grilled Fish

Ingredients:

- 4 oz white fish fillet (e.g., tilapia, cod, or your choice)

- 1 lemon, juiced

- 1 clove garlic, minced

- 1/2 teaspoon dried thyme

- 1/2 teaspoon dried oregano

- Salt and pepper to taste

- Olive oil for grilling

Procedure:

1. Lemon juice, minced garlic, dried oregano, dried thyme, and salt and pepper should all be combined in a bowl.

2. Transfer the fish fillet to a shallow dish and cover it with the marinade of lemon and herbs. Give it 15 to 30 minutes to marinate.

3. Turn the heat up to medium-high and coat your grill with a thin layer of olive oil.

4. The fish should have grill marks and flake easily after grilling it for 4–5 minutes on each side.

5. Savor the fresh flavors of the lemon herb grilled fish as it is served hot.

Time Frame:

- Preparation Time: 5 minutes

- Marinating Time: 15-30 minutes

- Grilling Time: 8-10 minutes

- Total Time: 28-45 minutes

Yield:

- 1 serving

Nutritional Value:

- Calories: 180

- Carbohydrates: 4g

- Protein: 30g

- Fat: 6g

- Fiber: 2g

- Sugar: 1g

4. Cauliflower Rice with Shrimp

Ingredients:

- 4 oz peeled and deveined shrimp

- 1 cup cauliflower rice

- 1/4 cup diced bell peppers (red, green, or yellow)

- 1/4 cup diced onions

- 1 clove garlic, minced

- 1/2 tablespoon olive oil

- 1/2 teaspoon paprika

- Salt and pepper to taste

Procedure:

1. Heat the olive oil in a skillet over medium-high heat.

2. Add the diced onions, bell peppers, and garlic, minced. Cook them until they are soft.

3. When the shrimp are pink and opaque, add them to the skillet and cook.

4. Mix in the paprika and cauliflower rice. Cook the cauliflower rice for a few more minutes, or until it's thoroughly heated.

5. To taste, add salt and pepper for seasoning.

6. Serve the shrimp over hot cauliflower rice, and savor a tasty, low-carb dinner.

Time Frame:

- Preparation Time: 10 minutes

- Cooking Time: 10 minutes

- Total Time: 20 minutes

Yield:

- 1 serving

Nutritional Value:

- Calories: 250

- Carbohydrates: 10g

- Protein: 26g

- Fat: 11g

- Fiber: 4g

- Sugar: 4g

5. Zucchini Noodles with Pesto and Cherry Tomatoes

Ingredients:

- 1 medium zucchini, spiralized into noodles

- 1/2 cup cherry tomatoes, halved

- 2 tablespoons pesto sauce

- 1 tablespoon grated Parmesan cheese

- Salt and pepper to taste

- Olive oil for sautéing

Procedure:

1. Heat the olive oil in a skillet over medium-high heat.

2. Add the cherry tomatoes and zucchini noodles. The tomatoes should be slightly blistered and the zucchini noodles should be soft after a few minutes of sautéing.

3. Add the pesto sauce and let it cook for an additional minute.

4. To taste, add salt and pepper for seasoning.

5. Sprinkle grated Parmesan cheese on top and serve the hot zucchini noodles with pesto and cherry tomatoes.

Time Frame:

- Preparation Time: 10 minutes

- Cooking Time: 5 minutes

- Total Time: 15 minutes

Yield:

- 1 serving

Nutritional Value:

- Calories: 280

- Carbohydrates: 12g

- Protein: 5g

- Fat: 24g

- Fiber: 3g

- Sugar: 6g

6. Quinoa and Black Bean Salad

Ingredients:

- 1/2 cup cooked quinoa

- 1/2 cup canned black beans, drained and rinsed

- 1/2 cup diced tomatoes

- 1/4 cup diced red onions

- 1/4 cup chopped fresh cilantro

- 1/2 lime, juiced

- 1/2 tablespoon olive oil

- Salt and pepper to taste

- Avocado slices (optional for garnish)

Procedure:

1. The cooked quinoa, black beans, chopped cilantro, diced tomatoes, and diced red onions should all be combined in a bowl.

2. Squeeze lime juice over the salad and drizzle with olive oil.

3. Add salt and pepper to taste and toss again to combine the ingredients.

4. If desired, garnish with slices of avocado.

5. For a cool, low-carb supper, serve the quinoa and black bean salad cold or room temperature.

Time Frame:

- Preparation Time: 10 minutes

- Total Time: 10 minutes

Yield:

- 1 serving

Nutritional Value:

- Calories: 300

- Carbohydrates: 51g

- Protein: 10g

- Fat: 7g

- Fiber: 13g

- Sugar: 3g

7. Balsamic Glazed Chicken

Ingredients:

- 4 oz boneless, skinless chicken breast

- 2 tablespoons balsamic vinegar

- 1/2 tablespoon olive oil

- 1 clove garlic, minced

- 1/2 teaspoon dried thyme

- Salt and pepper to taste

Procedure:

1. Balsamic vinegar, olive oil, dried thyme, minced garlic, salt, and pepper should all be combined in a bowl.

2. After putting the chicken breast in a shallow dish, cover it with the balsamic glaze. Give it 15 to 30 minutes to marinate.

3. Set the temperature of your skillet or grill to medium-high.

4. Cook the chicken on the grill or pan-sear it for 5 to 7 minutes on each side, or until it's cooked through and no longer has a pink center.

5. Drizzle any leftover glaze over the hot balsamic-glazed chicken before serving.

Time Frame:

- Preparation Time: 5 minutes

- Marinating Time: 15-30 minutes

- Cooking Time: 10-14 minutes

- Total Time: 30-49 minutes

Yield:

- 1 serving

Nutritional Value:

- Calories: 240

- Carbohydrates: 3g

- Protein: 28g

- Fat: 12g

- Fiber: 0g

- Sugar: 2g

8. Beef and Broccoli Stir-Fry

Ingredients:

- 4 oz lean beef (e.g., sirloin), thinly sliced

- 1 cup broccoli florets

- 1/4 cup low-sodium soy sauce

- 1 clove garlic, minced

- 1/2 tablespoon olive oil

- 1/2 tablespoon cornstarch

- Salt and pepper to taste

Procedure:

1. Mix the cornstarch, minced garlic, low-sodium soy sauce, salt, and pepper in a bowl.

2. Transfer the beef slices to a shallow dish and cover with the soy sauce mixture. Give it 15 to 30 minutes to marinate.

3. In a nonstick skillet set over medium-high heat, warm the olive oil.

4. When the broccoli florets are crisp-tender, add them and stir-fry for a few minutes.

5. After removing, place the broccoli aside.

6. Cook the marinated beef in the same skillet until it is no longer pink.

7. When the broccoli is back in the skillet, stir everything together.

8. Serve hot stir-fried beef and broccoli for a tasty, low-carb supper.

Time Frame:

- Preparation Time: 10 minutes

- Marinating Time: 15-30 minutes

- Cooking Time: 10 minutes

- Total Time: 35-50 minutes

Yield:

- 1 serving

Nutritional Value:

- Calories: 280

- Carbohydrates: 10g

- Protein: 26g

- Fat: 14g

- Fiber: 3g

- Sugar: 2g

9. Lemon Garlic Roasted Turkey

Ingredients:

- 4 oz turkey breast, boneless and skinless

- 1 lemon, juiced

- 1 clove garlic, minced

- 1/2 tablespoon olive oil

- 1/2 teaspoon dried rosemary

- Salt and pepper to taste

Procedure:

1. Whisk together the lemon juice, olive oil, dried rosemary, minced garlic, salt, and pepper.

2. Transfer the turkey breast to a shallow dish and cover it with the marinade of lemon and garlic. Give it 15 to 30 minutes to marinate.

3. Turn the oven on to 375°F, or 190°C.

4. After placing the turkey breast in a baking dish, roast it for 25 to 30 minutes, or until the juices run clear and the meat is thoroughly cooked.

5. For a flavorful and filling dinner, serve the turkey with garlic and lemon roasting hot.

Time Frame:

- Preparation Time: 5 minutes

- Marinating Time: 15-30 minutes

- Roasting Time: 25-30 minutes

- Total Time: 45-65 minutes

Yield:

- 1 serving

Nutritional Value:

- Calories: 260

- Carbohydrates: 2g

- Protein: 28g

- Fat: 14g

- Fiber: 1g

- Sugar: 0g

10. Spinach and Mushroom Stuffed Chicken Breast

Ingredients:

- 4 oz boneless, skinless chicken breast

- 1/4 cup fresh spinach, chopped

- 1/4 cup sliced mushrooms

- 1/4 cup low-fat mozzarella cheese

- 1/2 teaspoon Italian seasoning

- Salt and pepper to taste

- Olive oil for sautéing

Procedure:

1. Turn the oven on to 375°F, or 190°C.

2. Heat the olive oil in a skillet over medium-high heat.

3. Sliced mushrooms should be added and sautéed until they release moisture and soften.

4. Cook the chopped spinach until it wilts, stirring occasionally. Add salt, pepper, and Italian seasoning to taste.

5. Create a pocket in the chicken breast, then fill it with the mixture of spinach and mushrooms.

6. Top the chicken with low-fat mozzarella cheese.

7. The stuffed chicken breast should be placed in a baking dish and covered with foil.

8. Bake for 25 to 30 minutes, or until the cheese has melted and the chicken is thoroughly cooked.

9. Serve the delicious low-carb dish, stuffed chicken breast with spinach and mushrooms, hot.

Time Frame:

- Preparation Time: 20 minutes

- Baking Time: 25-30 minutes

- Total Time: 45-50 minutes

Yield:

- 1 serving

Nutritional Value:

- Calories: 280

- Carbohydrates: 5g

- Protein: 32g

- Fat: 12g

- Fiber: 2g

- Sugar: 2g

Five Healthy Snacks and Appetizers

1. Hummus and Veggie Platter

Ingredients:

- 2 tablespoons hummus

- Assorted fresh vegetables (carrot sticks, cucumber slices, bell pepper strips)

- Cherry tomatoes for garnish

- Olive oil for drizzling (optional)

- Fresh herbs for garnish (e.g., parsley)

Procedure:

1. Place the assortment of fresh vegetables onto a serving dish.

2. A tiny bowl of hummus for dipping should be placed in the middle.

3. Add fresh herbs and cherry tomatoes as garnish.

4. For extra flavor, feel free to drizzle with a little olive oil.

5. Present the veggie and hummus platter as a nutritious and eye-catching snack.

Time Frame:

- Preparation Time: 10 minutes

- Total Time: 10 minutes

Yield:

- 1 serving

Nutritional Value:

- Calories: 150

- Carbohydrates: 15g

- Protein: 6g

- Fat: 8g

- Fiber: 6g

- Sugar: 6g

2. Spiced Nuts

Ingredients:

- 1/4 cup mixed unsalted nuts (e.g., almonds, walnuts, cashews)

- 1/2 teaspoon ground cinnamon

- 1/4 teaspoon ground cayenne pepper (adjust to your spice preference)

- 1/2 teaspoon olive oil (for roasting)

- Salt to taste

Procedure:

1. Set the oven temperature to 350°F (175°C).

2. Combine the mixed nuts, salt, ground cayenne, ground cinnamon, and olive oil in a bowl.

3. Arrange the roasted almonds onto a baking sheet.

4. Roast for ten to fifteen minutes, or until fragrant and just toasted, in an oven that has been preheated.

5. Let cool completely before serving.

6. Savor this crunchy and filling snack of spiced nuts.

Time Frame:

- Preparation Time: 5 minutes

- Baking Time: 10-15 minutes

- Total Time: 15-20 minutes

Yield:

- 1 serving

Nutritional Value:

- Calories: 220

- Carbohydrates: 6g

- Protein: 7g

- Fat: 19g

- Fiber: 4g

- Sugar: 1g

3. Guacamole with Whole Wheat Pita

Ingredients:

- 1 ripe avocado

- 1/4 cup diced tomatoes

- 2 tablespoons diced onions

- 1 clove garlic, minced

- 1/2 lime, juiced

- Salt and pepper to taste

- Whole wheat pita, cut into wedges for dipping

Procedure:

1. Mash the ripe avocado in a bowl.

2. Add the lime juice, minced garlic, diced tomatoes, and diced onions.

3. After thoroughly combining, add salt and pepper to taste.

4. Present the guacamole alongside whole wheat pita wedges for a nutritious and delectable appetizer.

Time Frame:

- Preparation Time: 10 minutes

- Total Time: 10 minutes

Yield

- 1 serving

Nutritional Value:

- Calories: 250

- Carbohydrates: 21g

- Protein: 4g

- Fat: 17g

- Fiber: 9g

- Sugar: 3g

4. Caprese Skewers

Ingredients:

- Cherry tomatoes

- Fresh mozzarella balls

- Fresh basil leaves

- Balsamic glaze for drizzling (optional)

- Toothpicks for skewering

Procedure:

1. Using a toothpick, thread a cherry tomato, a fresh mozzarella ball, and a fresh basil leaf.

2. Continue doing this until you have several skewers.

3. Drizzle with balsamic glaze, if desired, to add more flavor.

4. Present the caprese skewers as a tasty and revitalizing snack.

appetizer.

Time Frame:

- Preparation Time: 10 minutes

- Total Time: 10 minutes

Yield:

- 1 serving

Nutritional Value:

- Calories: 180

- Carbohydrates: 5g

- Protein: 14g

- Fat: 12g

- Fiber: 1g

- Sugar: 2g

5. Baked Sweet Potato Fries

Ingredients:

- 1 small sweet potato, cut into fries

- 1/2 tablespoon olive oil

- 1/4 teaspoon paprika

- Salt and pepper to taste

Procedure:

1. Set the oven temperature to 425°F (220°C).

2. Combine the sweet potato fries, olive oil, paprika, salt, and pepper in a bowl.

3. Arrange the fries with seasoning on a baking sheet.

4. Roast for about 20 to 25 minutes, or until crispy and golden, in a preheated oven.

5. Before serving, allow them to cool slightly.

6. Savor this delicious and guilt-free snack of baked sweet potato fries.

Time Frame:

- Preparation Time: 10 minutes

- Baking Time: 20-25 minutes

- Total Time: 30-35 minutes

Yield:

- 1 serving

Nutritional Value:

- Calories: 220

- Carbohydrates: 26g

- Protein: 2g

- Fat: 12g

- Fiber: 4g

- Sugar: 5g

6. Greek Yogurt Dip with Sliced Cucumbers

Ingredients:

- 1/2 cup Greek yogurt

- 1/4 cucumber, sliced into rounds

- 1/2 teaspoon fresh dill, chopped

- 1/4 teaspoon lemon zest

- Salt and pepper to taste

Procedure:

1. Greek yogurt, lemon zest, fresh dill, salt, and pepper should all be combined in a bowl.

2. Mix the blend thoroughly.

3. Serve the protein-rich and refreshing Greek yogurt dip with sliced cucumbers.

Time Frame:

- Preparation Time: 5 minutes

- Total Time: 5 minutes

Yield:

- 1 serving

Nutritional Value:

- Calories: 90

- Carbohydrates: 8g

- Protein: 12g

- Fat: 1g

- Fiber: 1g

- Sugar: 5g

7. Salsa and Baked Tortilla Chips

Ingredients:

- Whole wheat tortilla chips (store-bought or homemade)

- Salsa (sugar-free or low-sugar)

Procedure:

1. To make your own tortilla chips, preheat your oven to 350°F (175°C).

2. Whole wheat tortillas should be cut into wedges and put on a baking sheet.

3. The tortilla chips should be baked for 8 to 10 minutes, or until they are lightly golden and crisp.

4. Let the chips cool down.

5. Serve with salsa on the side for a filling and guilt-free munchie.

Time Frame:

- Preparation Time: 5 minutes (for homemade tortilla chips)

- Baking Time: 8-10 minutes (for homemade tortilla chips)

- Total Time: 13-15 minutes (for homemade tortilla chips)

Yield:

- 1 serving

Nutritional Value:

- Calories: 180

- Carbohydrates: 30g

- Protein: 4g

- Fat: 4g

- Fiber: 6g

- Sugar: 2g

8. Stuffed Mushrooms with Spinach and Feta

Ingredients:

- 4 large mushrooms, cleaned and stems removed

- 1/4 cup chopped spinach

- 1/4 cup crumbled feta cheese

- 1/2 clove garlic, minced

- Olive oil for drizzling

- Salt and pepper to taste

Procedure:

1. Turn the oven on to 375°F, or 190°C.

2. Add minced garlic, feta cheese crumbles, chopped spinach, salt, and pepper to a bowl.

3. Incorporate the spinach and feta mixture into the mushroom caps.

4. After stuffing the mushrooms, transfer them to a baking dish and cover with olive oil.

5. Bake for 20 to 25 minutes, until the filling is golden, and bubbly and the mushrooms are soft.

6. Warm stuffed mushrooms with spinach and feta make a flavorful and filling snack.

Time Frame:

- Preparation Time: 10 minutes

- Baking Time: 20-25 minutes

- Total Time: 30-35 minutes

Yield:

- 1 serving

Nutritional Value:

- Calories: 170

- Carbohydrates: 6g

- Protein: 9g

- Fat: 12g

- Fiber: 2g

- Sugar: 3g

9. Edamame with Sea Salt

Ingredients:

- 1/2 cup edamame (steamed or boiled)

- Sea salt for seasoning

Procedure:

1. Edamame should be boiled or steamed until soft.

2. To taste, add a sprinkle of sea salt.

3. Serve edamame as a high-protein, nutrient-dense snack.

Time Frame:

- Preparation Time: 5 minutes

- Cooking Time: 5 minutes

- Total Time: 10 minutes

Yield:

- 1 serving

Nutritional Value:

- Calories: 90

- Carbohydrates: 7g

- Protein: 8g

- Fat: 3g

- Fiber: 3g

- Sugar: 1g

10. Crispy Baked Chickpeas

Ingredients:

- 1/2 cup canned chickpeas, drained and rinsed

- 1/2 tablespoon olive oil

- 1/4 teaspoon ground cumin

- 1/4 teaspoon paprika

- Salt and pepper to taste

Procedure:

1. Set oven temperature to 400°F, or 200°C.

2. Combine the chickpeas, paprika, ground cumin, olive oil, salt, and pepper in a bowl.

3. Arrange the savory chickpeas onto a baking tray.

4. Roast for about 20 to 25 minutes, or until crispy and golden, in a preheated oven.

5. Let cool completely before serving.

6. Savor this crunchy, high-protein snack of crispy baked chickpeas.

Time Frame:

- Preparation Time: 5 minutes

- Baking Time: 20-25 minutes

- Total Time: 25-30 minutes

Yield:

- 1 serving

Nutritional Value:

- Calories: 200

- Carbohydrates: 30g

- Protein: 9g

- Fat: 6g

- Fiber: 7g

- Sugar: 5g

Vegetable And Side Dishes

1. Roasted Garlic Asparagus

Ingredients:

- 1 bunch of fresh asparagus spears

- 1-2 cloves garlic, minced

- 1/2 tablespoon olive oil

- Salt and pepper to taste

- Lemon zest (optional, for garnish)

Procedure:

1. Set the oven temperature to 425°F (220°C).

2. Snip off the asparagus spears' tough ends.

3. Combine the asparagus, olive oil, salt, and pepper in a bowl along with the minced garlic.

4. Arrange the asparagus, spiced side down, on a baking sheet.

5. Roast the asparagus for 12 to 15 minutes, or until it's soft and starting to caramelize, in a preheated oven.

6. If desired, garnish with lemon zest.

7. Serve the flavorful and nutrient-dense roasted garlic asparagus as a side dish.

Time Frame:

- Preparation Time: 10 minutes

- Roasting Time: 12-15 minutes

- Total Time: 22-25 minutes

Yield:

- 1 serving

Nutritional Value:

- Calories: 80

- Carbohydrates: 8g

- Protein: 4g

- Fat: 5g

- Fiber: 4g

- Sugar: 2g

2. Cabbage and Carrot Coleslaw

Ingredients:

- 1 cup shredded green cabbage

- 1/2 cup shredded carrots

- 2 tablespoons low-fat Greek yogurt

- 1/2 tablespoon apple cider vinegar

- 1/4 teaspoon honey (optional)

- Salt and pepper to taste

Procedure:

1. Shredded carrots and green cabbage should be combined in a bowl.

2. Low-fat Greek yogurt, apple cider vinegar, honey (if using), salt, and pepper should all be combined in a different bowl.

3. Drizzle the cabbage and carrot mixture with the dressing, then toss to coat.

4. As a zesty and crunchy side dish, present the cabbage and carrot coleslaw.

Time Frame:

- Preparation Time: 10 minutes

- Total Time: 10 minutes

Yield:

- 1 serving

Nutritional Value:

- Calories: 90

- Carbohydrates: 16g

- Protein: 4g

- Fat: 2g

- Fiber: 5g

- Sugar: 9g

3. Lemon Herb Quinoa

Ingredients:

- 1/2 cup cooked quinoa

- 1/2 lemon, juiced

- 1/2 tablespoon olive oil

- 1/2 teaspoon dried herbs (e.g., basil, oregano, thyme)

- Salt and pepper to taste

Procedure:

1. The cooked quinoa, lemon juice, olive oil, dried herbs, salt, and pepper should all be combined in a bowl.

2. Toss to combine the contents.

3. Serve the quinoa with lemon and herbs as a healthy and flavorful side dish.

Time Frame:

- Preparation Time: 10 minutes (if quinoa is pre-cooked)

- Total Time: 10 minutes

Yield:

- 1 serving

Nutritional Value:

- Calories: 150

- Carbohydrates: 25g

- Protein: 4g

- Fat: 4g

- Fiber: 3g

- Sugar: 1g

4. Ratatouille

Ingredients:

- 1 small eggplant, cubed

- 1 small zucchini, sliced

- 1 small yellow bell pepper, chopped

- 1 small red onion, chopped

- 1/2 cup diced tomatoes

- 1 clove garlic, minced

- 1/2 tablespoon olive oil

- Dried herbs (e.g., basil, thyme, rosemary)

- Salt and pepper to taste

Procedure:

1. Heat the olive oil in a skillet over medium-high heat.

2. Add the minced garlic and cook for a short while.

3. Add the diced tomatoes, red onion, yellow bell pepper, eggplant, and zucchini.

4. Add salt, pepper, and dried herbs for seasoning.

5. Simmer for 15 to 20 minutes, or until the veggies are soft and the flavors have blended.

6. Serve the ratatouille as a filling side dish with a Mediterranean flair.

Time Frame:

- Preparation Time: 15 minutes

- Cooking Time: 15-20 minutes

- Total Time: 30-35 minutes

Yield:

- 1 serving

Nutritional Value:

- Calories: 160

- Carbohydrates: 30g

- Protein: 5g

- Fat: 4g

- Fiber: 8g

- Sugar: 10g

5. Steamed Broccoli with Almonds

Ingredients:

- 1 cup broccoli florets

- 1 tablespoon slivered almonds

- 1/2 tablespoon olive oil

- Lemon juice for drizzling

- Salt and pepper to taste

Procedure:

1. Broccoli florets should be steamed until they are crisp-tender.

2. Heat the olive oil in a skillet over medium-high heat.

3. Almond slivers should be added and gently toasted until they turn golden.

4. Add the toasted almonds to the steamed broccoli and toss to coat. Season with salt, pepper, and lemon juice.

5. Steamed broccoli is a tasty and nutritious side dish when served with almonds.

Time Frame:

- Preparation Time: 10 minutes

- Cooking Time: 5 minutes

- Total Time: 15 minutes

Yield:

- 1 serving

Nutritional Value:

- Calories: 90

- Carbohydrates: 8g

- Protein: 4g

- Fat: 6g

- Fiber: 3g

- Sugar: 2g

6. Baked Brussels Sprouts

Ingredients:

- 1 cup Brussels sprouts, trimmed and halved

- 1/2 tablespoon olive oil

- 1/2 teaspoon balsamic vinegar (optional)

- Salt and pepper to taste

Procedure:

1. Set oven temperature to 400°F, or 200°C.

2. Add salt, pepper, olive oil, and balsamic vinegar (if using) to the chopped and halved Brussels sprouts.

3. On a baking sheet, distribute the seasoned Brussels sprouts.

4. Bake for about 20 to 25 minutes, or until the edges are crispy and the center is still soft, in a preheated oven.

5. Baked Brussels sprouts make a tasty and high-fiber side dish.

Time Frame:

- Preparation Time: 10 minutes

- Baking Time: 20-25 minutes

- Total Time: 30-35 minutes

Yield:

- 1 serving

Nutritional Value:

- Calories: 90

- Carbohydrates: 10g

- Protein: 3g

- Fat: 5g

- Fiber: 4g

- Sugar: 3g

7. Green Beans with Garlic and Lemon

Ingredients:

- 1 cup green beans, trimmed

- 1 clove garlic, minced

- 1/2 lemon, juiced

- 1/2 tablespoon olive oil

- Salt and pepper to taste

Procedure:

1. Green beans should be steamed until they are crisp-tender.

2. Heat the olive oil in a skillet over medium-high heat.

3. Add the minced garlic and quickly sauté it.

4. Stir in the steamed green beans and season with salt, pepper, and lemon juice.

5. Serve the green beans as a bright and colorful side dish with garlic and lemon.

Time Frame:

- Preparation Time: 10 minutes

- Cooking Time: 5 minutes

- Total Time: 15 minutes

Yield:

- 1 serving

Nutritional Value:

- Calories: 70

- Carbohydrates: 10g

- Protein: 2g

- Fat: 3g

- Fiber: 4g

- Sugar: 2g

8. Mashed Cauliflower

Ingredients:

- 1 cup cauliflower florets

- 1/2 tablespoon low-fat Greek yogurt

- 1/2 tablespoon grated Parmesan cheese

- Salt and pepper to taste

Procedure:

1. The cauliflower florets should be steamed until tender.

2. Mash the steamed cauliflower with grated Parmesan cheese, low-fat Greek yogurt, salt, and pepper in a bowl.

3. Serve the mashed cauliflower as a low-carb, creamy substitute for the mashed potatoes.

Time Frame:

- Preparation Time: 10 minutes

- Cooking Time: 5 minutes

- Total Time: 15 minutes

Yield:

- 1 serving

Nutritional Value:

- Calories: 70

- Carbohydrates: 7g

- Protein: 5g

- Fat: 3g

- Fiber: 4g

- Sugar: 3g

9. Stuffed Bell Peppers with Quinoa

Ingredients:

- 1 bell pepper, halved and cleaned

- 1/4 cup cooked quinoa

- 1/4 cup black beans, drained and rinsed

- 1/4 cup diced tomatoes

- 1/4 teaspoon chili powder

- Salt and pepper to taste

Procedure:

1. Turn the oven on to 375°F, or 190°C.

2. Cooked quinoa, diced tomatoes, black beans, chili powder, salt, and pepper should all be combined in a bowl.

3. Fill the bell pepper halves with the mixture of quinoa.

4. The stuffed bell peppers should be put on a baking dish.

5. Bake the peppers for 20 to 25 minutes, or until they are soft.

6. Present the filled bell peppers alongside quinoa as a healthful and high-protein side dish.

Time Frame:

- Preparation Time: 10 minutes

- Baking Time: 20-25 minutes

- Total Time: 30-35 minutes

Yield:

- 1 serving

Nutritional Value:

- Calories: 180

- Carbohydrates: 30g

- Protein: 7g

- Fat: 2g

- Fiber: 9g

- Sugar: 4g

10. Cilantro Lime Brown Rice

Ingredients:

- 1/2 cup cooked brown rice

- 1/2 lime, juiced

- 1 tablespoon fresh cilantro, chopped

- Salt and pepper to taste

Procedure:

1. Cooked brown rice, lime juice, fresh cilantro, salt, and pepper should all be combined in a bowl.

2. Toss to combine the contents.

3. Present the brown rice with cilantro and lime as a flavorful and high-fiber side dish.

Time Frame:

- Preparation Time: 10 minutes (if rice is pre-cooked)

- Total Time: 10 minutes

Yield:

- 1 serving

Nutritional Value:

- Calories: 120

- Carbohydrates: 26g

- Protein: 3g

- Fat: 1g

- Fiber: 3g

- Sugar: 0g

Diabetic-Friendly Chicken and Turkey Recipes

1. Chicken and Vegetable Curry

Ingredients:

- 1 boneless, skinless chicken breast, cubed

- 1 cup mixed vegetables (e.g., bell peppers, carrots, broccoli)

- 1/2 cup low-sodium chicken broth

- 1/4 cup light coconut milk

- 1 tablespoon curry powder

- 1 clove garlic, minced

- 1/2 tablespoon olive oil

- Salt and pepper to taste

Procedure:

1. Heat the olive oil in a skillet over medium-high heat.

2. Chicken cubes should be added and sautéed until lightly browned.

3. After adding the chopped garlic, curry powder, and mixed veggies, cook for a few more minutes.

4. Pour in light coconut milk and low-sodium chicken broth. Add pepper and salt for seasoning.

5. Simmer until the veggies are soft and the chicken is cooked through.

6. Serve this low-carb, flavorful chicken and vegetable curry.

Time Frame:

- Preparation Time: 10 minutes

- Cooking Time: 20 minutes

- Total Time: 30 minutes

Yield:

- 1 serving

Nutritional Value:

- Calories: 280

- Carbohydrates: 18g

- Protein: 30g

- Fat: 9g

- Fiber: 5g

- Sugar: 6g

2. Teriyaki Turkey Tenderloin

Ingredients:

- 1 turkey tenderloin

- 1/4 cup low-sodium teriyaki sauce

- 1/2 tablespoon honey (optional)

- 1/2 teaspoon grated ginger

- Salt and pepper to taste

Procedure:

1. Combine the low-sodium teriyaki sauce, grated ginger, honey (if using), salt, and pepper in a bowl.

2. For a minimum of half an hour, marinate the turkey tenderloin in the mixture.

3. Brush the turkey tenderloin with marinade as it cooks and grill or roast it until it's done.

4. Present the tender and flavorful turkey tenderloin with teriyaki sauce.

Time Frame:

- Preparation Time: 5 minutes

- Cooking Time: 20-25 minutes

- Total Time: 25-30 minutes (including marinating time)

Yield:

- 1 servi

Nutritional Value:

- Calories: 200

- Carbohydrates: 8g

- Protein: 30g

- Fat: 4g

- Fiber: 1g

- Sugar: 5g

3. Lemon Herb Roasted Chicken

Ingredients:

- 1 chicken breast, bone-in and skin-on

- 1/2 lemon, juiced

- 1/2 tablespoon olive oil

- 1/2 teaspoon dried herbs (e.g., thyme, rosemary, oregano)

- Salt and pepper to taste

Procedure:

1. Turn the oven on to 375°F, or 190°C.

2. Combine the lemon juice, olive oil, salt, pepper, and dried herbs in a bowl.

3. Apply the lemon-herb mixture to the chicken breast.

4. Roast for about 25 to 30 minutes, or until the skin is crispy and the chicken is cooked through, in a preheated oven.

5. Present the roasted chicken with lemon and herbs as a flavorful and high-protein dish.

Time Frame:

- Preparation Time: 10 minutes

- Roasting Time: 25-30 minutes

- Total Time: 35-40 minutes

Yield:

- 1 serving

Nutritional Value:

- Calories: 220

- Carbohydrates: 3g

- Protein: 30g

- Fat: 10g

- Fiber: 1g

- Sugar: 1g

4. Turkey Chili

Ingredients:

- 1/2 cup ground turkey

- 1/4 cup black beans, drained and rinsed

- 1/4 cup kidney beans, drained and rinsed

- 1/2 cup diced tomatoes

- 1/2 teaspoon chili powder

- 1/4 teaspoon cumin

- Salt and pepper to taste

Procedure:

1. Cook the ground turkey in a skillet until it's browned.

2. Add the kidney and black beans, diced tomatoes, cumin, chili powder, salt, and pepper.

3. Simmer for ten to fifteen minutes, or until the ingredients are thoroughly heated and the flavors have blended.

4. Serve the turkey chili as a satisfying, high-protein supper.

Time Frame:

- Preparation Time: 10 minutes

- Cooking Time: 15 minutes

- Total Time: 25 minutes

Yield:

- 1 serving

Nutritional Value:

- Calories: 290

- Carbohydrates: 23g

- Protein: 25g

- Fat: 8g

- Fiber: 8g

- Sugar: 6g

5. Garlic Parmesan Chicken Thighs

Ingredients:

- 2 boneless, skinless chicken thighs

- 1/2 tablespoon olive oil

- 1 clove garlic, minced

- 1/2 tablespoon grated Parmesan cheese

- Salt and pepper to taste

Procedure:

1. Heat the olive oil in a skillet over medium-high heat.

2. Add the minced garlic and cook for a short while.

3. Season with salt, pepper, and grated Parmesan cheese after adding the chicken thighs.

4. Cook for 12 to 15 minutes, or until the chicken is well cooked and browned.

5. Serve the chicken thighs with garlic and Parmesan cheese as a flavorful and filling meal.

Time Frame:

- Preparation Time: 5 minutes

- Cooking Time: 12-15 minutes

- Total Time: 17-20 minutes

Yield:

- 1 serving

Nutritional Value:

- Calories: 240

- Carbohydrates: 2g

- Protein: 30g

- Fat: 12g

- Fiber: 1g

- Sugar: 0g

6. Chicken and Spinach Soup

Ingredients:

- 1 boneless, skinless chicken breast, cubed

- 2 cups fresh spinach leaves

- 1/2 onion, diced

- 1 carrot, sliced

- 1 celery stalk, sliced

- 1 clove garlic, minced

- 4 cups low-sodium chicken broth

- Salt and pepper to taste

Procedure:

1. Diced onion and minced garlic should be sautéed in a pot until fragrant.

2. Stir in the celery, carrot, and cubed chicken. Cook until there is a light browning on the chicken.

3. Add the low-sodium chicken broth and simmer for a while.

4. Cook the spinach until it wilts after adding fresh spinach.

5. Add pepper and salt for seasoning.

6. Serve the low-carb and nutritious chicken and spinach soup.

Time Frame:

- Preparation Time: 10 minutes

- Cooking Time: 20 minutes

- Total Time: 30 minutes

Yield:

- 1 serving

Nutritional Value:

- Calories: 200

- Carbohydrates: 10g

- Protein: 30g

- Fat: 3g

- Fiber: 3g

- Sugar: 4g

7. BBQ Turkey Drumsticks

Ingredients:

- 2 turkey drumsticks

- 1/4 cup sugar-free BBQ sauce

- 1/2 tablespoon olive oil

- Salt and pepper to taste

Procedure:

1. Turn the oven on to 375°F, or 190°C.

2. Combine olive oil, sugar-free BBQ sauce, salt, and pepper in a bowl.

3. Apply the BBQ mixture to the drumsticks of turkey.

4. Roast for about 30 to 35 minutes, or until the skin is crispy and the turkey is cooked through.

5. Serve the flavorful and high-protein BBQ turkey drumsticks.

Time Frame:

- Preparation Time: 5 minutes

- Cooking Time: 30-35 minutes

- Total Time: 35-40 minutes

Yield:

- 1 serving

Nutritional Value:

- Calories: 250

- Carbohydrates: 5g

- Protein: 30g

- Fat: 12g

- Fiber: 0g

- Sugar: 3g

8. Chicken and Asparagus Stir-Fry

Ingredients:

- 1 boneless, skinless chicken breast, sliced

- 1 cup asparagus, cut into bite-sized pieces

- 1/2 red bell pepper, sliced

- 1/2 onion, sliced

- 1 clove garlic, minced

- 1/2 tablespoon low-sodium soy sauce

- 1/2 tablespoon olive oil

- Salt and pepper to taste

Procedure:

1. Heat the olive oil in a skillet over medium-high heat.

2. When the chicken is well cooked and browned, add the slices and continue cooking.

3. Add the onion, red bell pepper, minced garlic, and asparagus. The vegetables should be stir-fried for a few minutes to make them soft.

4. Over the stir-fry, drizzle low-sodium soy sauce and toss.

5. Add pepper and salt for seasoning.

6. Serve the savory and nutrient-dense stir-fried chicken and asparagus as a meal.

Time Frame:

- Preparation Time: 10 minutes

- Cooking Time: 15 minutes

- Total Time: 25 minutes

Yield:

- 1 serving

Nutritional Value:

- Calories: 220

- Carbohydrates: 10g

- Protein: 30g

- Fat: 5g

- Fiber: 3g

- Sugar: 4g

9. Turkey and Sweet Potato Stew

Ingredients:

- 1/2 cup ground turkey

- 1 small sweet potato, diced

- 1/4 cup diced tomatoes

- 1/4 cup black beans, drained and rinsed

- 1/2 teaspoon chili powder

- Salt and pepper to taste

Procedure:

1. Cook the ground turkey in a pot until browned.

2. Add the diced tomatoes, sweet potatoes, chili powder, black beans, and salt and pepper.

3. Simmer for 20 to 25 minutes, or until the sweet potatoes are soft and the stew thickens.

4. Serve the stewed sweet potatoes and turkey as a filling, high-protein supper.

Time Frame:

- Preparation Time: 10 minutes

- Cooking Time: 20-25 minutes

- Total Time: 30-35 minutes

Yield:

- 1 serving

Nutritional Value:

- Calories: 280

- Carbohydrates: 30g

- Protein: 25g

- Fat: 6g

- Fiber: 7g

- Sugar: 6g

10. Lemon Garlic Chicken Breast

Ingredients:

- 1 chicken breast, boneless and skinless

- 1/2 lemon, juiced

- 1 clove garlic, minced

- 1/2 tablespoon olive oil

- Dried herbs (e.g., thyme, rosemary)

- Salt and pepper to taste

Procedure:

1. Combine the lemon juice, olive oil, dried herbs, minced garlic, salt, and pepper in a bowl.

2. Use the lemon-garlic mixture to lightly coat the chicken breast.

3. The chicken breast should be cooked through after grilling or roasting for 15 to 20 minutes.

4. Serve the lean and zesty chicken breast with garlic and lemon.

Time Frame:

- Preparation Time: 5 minutes

- Cooking Time: 15-20 minutes

- Total Time: 20-25 minutes

Yield:

- 1 serving

Nutritional Value:

- Calories: 220

- Carbohydrates: 2g

- Protein: 30g

- Fat: 9g

- Fiber: 1g

- Sugar: 0g

Lean Beef And Pork Dishes

1. Beef and Vegetable Soup

Ingredients:

- 1/2 cup lean beef, cubed

- 1 cup mixed vegetables (e.g., carrots, celery, bell peppers)

- 1/2 onion, diced

- 1 clove garlic, minced

- 4 cups low-sodium beef broth

- Salt and pepper to taste

Procedure:

1. Diced onion and minced garlic should be sautéed in a pot until fragrant.

2. When the lean beef is browned, add the cubed steak and cook it.

3. Stir in the low-sodium beef broth and mixed vegetables.

4. Simmer until the veggies are cooked and the beef is tender.

5. Add pepper and salt for seasoning.

6. Serve the low-carb beef and vegetable soup as a filling supper.

Time Frame:

- Preparation Time: 10 minutes

- Cooking Time: 20 minutes

- Total Time: 30 minutes

Yield:

- 1 serving

Nutritional Value:

- Calories: 250

- Carbohydrates: 15g

- Protein: 30g

- Fat: 7g

- Fiber: 4g

- Sugar: 5g

2. Pork Tenderloin with Apples

Ingredients:

- 1 pork tenderloin

- 1 small apple, sliced

- 1/2 tablespoon honey (optional)

- 1/2 tablespoon olive oil

- Salt and pepper to taste

Procedure:

1. Turn the oven on to 375°F, or 190°C.

2. Combine olive oil, salt, pepper, and honey (if using) in a bowl.

3. Drizzle the mixture over the pork tenderloin and garnish with apple slices.

4. Roast for 25 to 30 minutes in a preheated oven, or until the pork is tender and the apples have a caramelized color.

5. Serve the pork tenderloin as a savory and sweet dish with apples.

Time Frame:

- Preparation Time: 5 minutes

- Cooking Time: 25-30 minutes

- Total Time: 30-35 minutes

Yield:

- 1 serving

Nutritional Value:

- Calories: 220

- Carbohydrates: 10g

- Protein: 30g

- Fat: 5g

- Fiber: 2g

- Sugar: 7g

3. Beef and Cabbage Stew

Ingredients:

- 1/2 cup lean ground beef

- 1 cup cabbage, sliced

- 1/2 onion, diced

- 1/2 clove garlic, minced

- 4 cups low-sodium beef broth

- 1/2 teaspoon paprika

- Salt and pepper to taste

Procedure:

1. Cook the lean ground beef until browned in a pot.

2. Add minced garlic and chopped onion. Briefly sauté.

3. Add the paprika and sliced cabbage.

4. Add the reduced-sodium beef broth.

5. Simmer until the cabbage is tender and the beef is cooked.

6. Add pepper and salt for seasoning.

7. Serve the stew of beef and cabbage as a filling, low-carb choice.

Time Frame:

- Preparation Time: 10 minutes

- Cooking Time: 20 minutes

- Total Time: 30 minutes

Yield:

- 1 serving

Nutritional Value:

- Calories: 250

- Carbohydrates: 12g

- Protein: 30g

- Fat: 8g

- Fiber: 4g

- Sugar: 6g

4. Spiced Pulled Pork

Ingredients:

- 1/2 cup pulled pork

- 1/4 teaspoon cumin

- 1/4 teaspoon paprika

- 1/4 teaspoon chili powder

- Salt and pepper to taste

Procedure:

1. Pull pork is heated in a skillet with cumin, paprika, chili powder, salt, and pepper added.

2. Sauté the pulled pork until it's thoroughly heated and the spices are evenly distributed.

3. Serve the flavorful and high protein pulled pork with spices.

Time Frame:

- Preparation Time: 5 minutes

- Cooking Time: 10 minutes

- Total Time: 15 minutes

Yield:

- 1 serving

Nutritional Value:

- Calories: 240

- Carbohydrates: 4g

- Protein: 30g

- Fat: 10g

- Fiber: 1g

- Sugar: 2g

5. Beef and Bell Pepper Stir-Fry

Ingredients:

- 1/2 cup lean beef strips

- 1 bell pepper, sliced

- 1/2 onion, sliced

- 1/2 clove garlic, minced

- 1/2 tablespoon low-sodium soy sauce

- 1/2 tablespoon olive oil

- Salt and pepper to taste

Procedure:

1. Heat the olive oil in a skillet over medium-high heat.

2. Cook the lean beef strips until they get browned.

3. Add the minced garlic, onion, and bell pepper slices. Until the veggies are soft, stir-fry them.

4. Over the stir-fry, drizzle low-sodium soy sauce and toss.

5. Add pepper and salt for seasoning.

6. Serve the low-carb, flavorful stir-fried beef and bell pepper.

Time Frame:

- Preparation Time: 10 minutes

- Cooking Time: 15 minutes

- Total Time: 25 minutes

Yield:

- 1 serving

Nutritional Value:

- Calories: 230

- Carbohydrates: 10g

- Protein: 30g

- Fat: 6g

- Fiber: 3g

- Sugar: 6g

6. Pork and Butternut Squash Chili

Ingredients:

- 1/2 cup ground pork

- 1 cup butternut squash, diced

- 1/4 cup black beans, drained and rinsed

- 1/4 cup diced tomatoes

- 1/2 teaspoon chili powder

- Salt and pepper to taste

Procedure:

1. The ground pork should be cooked in a pot until browned.

2. Add the diced tomatoes, black beans, chili powder, salt, and pepper along with the diced butternut squash.

3. Simmer for 20 to 25 minutes, or until the butternut squash is soft and the chili has thickened.

4. Serve the hearty, high-protein chili with pork and butternut squash.

Time Frame:

- Preparation Time: 10 minutes

- Cooking Time: 20-25 minutes

- Total Time: 30-35 minutes

Yield:

- 1 serving

Nutritional Value:

- Calories: 280

- Carbohydrates: 25g

- Protein: 25g

- Fat: 9g

- Fiber: 7g

- Sugar: 6g

7. Beef and Mushroom Skillet

Ingredients:

- 1/2 cup lean ground beef

- 1 cup mushrooms, sliced

- 1/2 onion, diced

- 1/2 clove garlic, minced

- 1/2 tablespoon olive oil

- Salt and pepper to taste

Procedure:

1. Heat the olive oil in a skillet over medium-high heat.

2. Cook the lean ground beef until it becomes browned.

3. Add the minced garlic, diced onion, and sliced mushrooms. Sauté the mushrooms until they become soft.

4. Add pepper and salt for seasoning.

5. Serve the skillet of beef and mushrooms as a tasty, low-carb supper.

Time Frame:

- Preparation Time: 10 minutes

- Cooking Time: 15 minutes

- Total Time: 25 minute

Yield:

- 1 serving

Nutritional Value:

- Calories: 250

- Carbohydrates: 8g

- Protein: 30g

- Fat: 10g

- Fiber: 3g

- Sugar: 4g

8. Pork and Broccoli Teriyaki

Ingredients:

- 1/2 cup lean ground pork

- 1 cup broccoli florets

- 1/2 clove garlic, minced

- 1/2 tablespoon low-sodium soy sauce

- 1/2 tablespoon honey (optional)

- Salt and pepper to taste

Procedure:

1. Cook lean ground pork until browned in a skillet.

2. Add the broccoli florets and minced garlic. Sauté the broccoli until it becomes soft.

3. Pour honey (if using) and low-sodium soy sauce over the pork and broccoli.

4. Add pepper and salt for seasoning.

5. Serve the teriyaki

Time Frame:

- Preparation Time: 10 minutes

- Cooking Time: 15 minutes

- Total Time: 25 minutes

Yield:

- 1 serving

Nutritional Value:

- Calories: 270

- Carbohydrates: 10g

- Protein: 30g

- Fat: 12g

- Fiber: 3g

- Sugar: 6g

9. Beef and Spinach Meatballs

Ingredients:

- 1/2 cup lean ground beef

- 1 cup fresh spinach leaves, chopped

- 1/2 onion, diced

- 1/2 clove garlic, minced

- 1/2 tablespoon whole wheat breadcrumbs

- Salt and pepper to taste

Procedure:

1. Lean ground beef, chopped spinach, diced onion, minced garlic, whole wheat breadcrumbs, salt, and pepper should all be combined in a bowl.

2. Shape the blend into meatballs.

3. Cook the meatballs in a skillet until they are thoroughly cooked and browned.

4. Serve the protein- and nutrient-rich beef and spinach meatballs as a healthy choice.

Time Frame:

- Preparation Time: 10 minutes

- Cooking Time: 15 minutes

- Total Time: 25 minutes

Yield:

- 1 serving

Nutritional Value:

- Calories: 260

- Carbohydrates: 10g

- Protein: 30g

- Fat: 10g

- Fiber: 4g

- Sugar: 5g

10. Pork and Cabbage Rolls

Ingredients:

- 2 cabbage leaves

- 1/2 cup lean ground pork

- 1/4 cup brown rice, cooked

- 1/4 cup diced tomatoes

- 1/2 clove garlic, minced

- Salt and pepper to taste

Procedure:

1. The cabbage leaves should be steamed until tender and supple.

2. Combine cooked brown rice, diced tomatoes, minced garlic, lean ground pork, salt, and pepper in a bowl.

3. Take a piece of the pork mixture and wrap it around each cabbage leaf.

4. Cook the cabbage rolls in a skillet until they are thoroughly heated.

5. Serve the cabbage and pork rolls as a filling, low-carb supper.

Time Frame:

- Preparation Time: 15 minutes

- Cooking Time: 15 minutes

- Total Time: 30 minutes

Yield:

- 1 serving

Nutritional Value:

- Calories: 290

- Carbohydrates: 20g

- Protein: 25g

- Fat: 8g

- Fiber: 4g

- Sugar: 5g

Fish And Seafood Dishes

1. Garlic Herb Grilled Shrimp

Ingredients:

- 8 large shrimp, peeled and deveined

- 2 cloves garlic, minced

- 1/2 lemon, juiced

- 1/2 tablespoon olive oil

- Fresh herbs (e.g., parsley, rosemary)

- Salt and pepper to taste

Procedure:

1. Combine the minced garlic, olive oil, lemon juice, fresh herbs, salt, and pepper in a bowl.

2. Apply the mixture to the shrimp and allow them to marinate for a short while.

3. The marinated shrimp should be cooked through and pink on the grill.

4. Serve the shrimp with garlic and herb grilling as a flavorful, high-protein dish.

Time Frame:

- Preparation Time: 10 minutes

- Grilling Time: 5-7 minutes

- Total Time: 15-17 minutes

Yield:

- 1 serving

Nutritional Value:

- Calories: 180

- Carbohydrates: 5g

- Protein: 25g

- Fat: 7g

- Fiber: 1g

- Sugar: 1g

2. Baked Salmon with Dill

Ingredients:

- 1 salmon fillet

- 1/2 lemon, juiced

- Fresh dill

- 1/2 tablespoon olive oil

- Salt and pepper to taste

Procedure:

1. Turn the oven on to 375°F, or 190°C.

2. Salmon fillet should be placed in a baking dish.

3. Pour olive oil and lemon juice over the salmon.

4. Season with salt, pepper, and fresh dill.

5. Bake for 15 to 20 minutes, or until the salmon is cooked through and flake easily, in a preheated oven.

6. As a tasty and high-omega-3 dish, serve the baked salmon with dill.

Time Frame:

- Preparation Time: 5 minutes

- Baking Time: 15-20 minutes

- Total Time: 20-25 minutes

Yield:

- 1 serving

Nutritional Value:

- Calories: 220

- Carbohydrates: 2g

- Protein: 30g

- Fat: 10g

- Fiber: 1g

- Sugar: 0g

3. Teriyaki Tuna Steaks

Ingredients:

- 1 tuna steak

- 1/2 cup low-sodium teriyaki sauce

- 1/2 tablespoon olive oil

- 1/2 clove garlic, minced

- Salt and pepper to taste

Procedure:

1. Combine the olive oil, minced garlic, low-sodium teriyaki sauce, salt, and pepper in a bowl.

2. Apply the teriyaki mixture to the tuna steak and allow it to marinate for a few minutes.

3. Use a skillet or grill to preheat it to medium-high.

4. To your desired doneness, cook the marinated tuna steak.

5. Serve the protein-rich and flavorful teriyaki tuna steak.

Time Frame:

- Preparation Time: 10 minutes

- Cooking Time: 5-7 minutes

- Total Time: 15-17 minutes

Yield:

- 1 serving

Nutritional Value:

- Calories: 240

- Carbohydrates: 12g

- Protein: 25g

- Fat: 8g

- Fiber: 0g

- Sugar: 7g

4. Lemon Garlic Tilapia

Ingredients:

- 1 tilapia fillet

- 1/2 lemon, juiced

- 1/2 tablespoon olive oil

- 1/2 clove garlic, minced

- Fresh herbs (e.g., parsley, thyme)

- Salt and pepper to taste

Procedure:

1. Turn the oven on to 375°F, or 190°C.

2. Tilapia fillet should be placed in a baking dish.

3. Over the tilapia, drizzle with olive oil, lemon juice, and minced garlic.

4. Season with salt, pepper, and fresh herbs.

5. Bake for 10 to 12 minutes, or until the tilapia is cooked through and flake easily, in a preheated oven.

6. Serve the tangy and low-calorie lemon garlic tilapia.

Time Frame:

- Preparation Time: 5 minutes

- Baking Time: 10-12 minutes

- Total Time: 15-17 minutes

Yield:

- 1 serving

Nutritional Value:

- Calories: 180

- Carbohydrates: 5g

- Protein: 25g

- Fat: 7g

- Fiber: 1g

- Sugar: 2g

5. Cajun Shrimp and Sausage

Ingredients:

- 8 large shrimp, peeled and deveined

- 1/2 smoked turkey sausage, sliced

- 1/2 bell pepper, sliced

- 1/2 onion, sliced

- Cajun seasoning

- 1/2 tablespoon olive oil

- Salt and pepper to taste

Procedure:

1. Heat the olive oil in a skillet over medium-high heat.

2. Add bell pepper, onion, sliced turkey sausage, and Cajun seasoning. Saute the sausage until it browns and the vegetables become soft.

3. When the shrimp are fully cooked and turn pink, add the peeled ones and continue cooking.

4. Add pepper and salt for seasoning.

5. Present the spicy and high-protein Cajun shrimp and sausage dish.

Time Frame:

- Preparation Time: 10 minutes

- Cooking Time: 10 minutes

- Total Time: 20 minutes

Yield:

- 1 serving

Nutritional Value:

- Calories: 220

- Carbohydrates: 10g

- Protein: 25g

- Fat: 10g

- Fiber: 3g

- Sugar: 4g

6. Coconut-Crusted Cod

Ingredients:

- 1 cod fillet

- 2 tablespoons unsweetened shredded coconut

- 1/2 lemon, juiced

- 1/2 tablespoon olive oil

- Salt and pepper to taste

Procedure:

1. Turn the oven on to 375°F, or 190°C.

2. Olive oil, lemon juice, salt, pepper, and unsweetened shredded coconut should all be combined in a bowl.

3. Apply the coconut mixture to the cod fillet.

4. The coated cod should be put in a baking dish.

5. Bake for 15 to 20 minutes, or until the coconut is golden brown and the cod is thoroughly cooked, in a preheated oven.

6. Present the coconut-crusted cod as a heart-healthy and tropical dish.

Time Frame:

- Preparation Time: 10 minutes

- Baking Time: 15-20 minutes

- Total Time: 25-30 minutes

Yield:

- 1 serving

Nutritional Value:

- Calories: 220

- Carbohydrates: 5g

- Protein: 25g

- Fat: 12g

- Fiber: 3g

- Sugar: 2g

7. Broiled Lemon Herb Trout

Ingredients:

- 1 trout fillet

- 1/2 lemon, juiced

- Fresh herbs (e.g., rosemary, thyme)

- 1/2 tablespoon olive oil

- Salt and pepper to taste

Procedure:

1. Warm up the broiler.

2. Put the trout fillet in a baking dish.

3. Pour olive oil, lemon juice, and fresh herbs on top of the trout.

4. Add pepper and salt for seasoning.

5. The trout should flake easily and be cooked through after about 10 to 12 minutes under the broiler.

6. Serve the zesty and omega-3-rich broiled lemon-herb trout.

Time Frame:

- Preparation Time: 5 minutes

- Broiling Time: 10-12 minutes

- Total Time: 15-17 minutes

Yield:

- 1 serving

Nutritional Value:

- Calories: 200

- Carbohydrates: 3g

- Protein: 25g

- Fat: 10g

- Fiber: 1g

- Sugar: 1g

8. Garlic Butter Scallops

Ingredients:

- 6 large scallops

- 1/2 clove garlic, minced

- 1/2 tablespoon unsalted butter

- Fresh parsley, chopped

- Salt and pepper to taste

Procedure:

1. Melt unsalted butter in a skillet over a medium-high heat.

2. When fragrant, add the minced garlic and sauté it.

3. When the scallops are opaque and seared, add them and cook.

4. Add salt, pepper, and fresh parsley on top.

5. Serve the protein-rich and luscious garlic butter scallops as a dish.

Time Frame:

- Preparation Time: 5 minutes

- Cooking Time: 5-7 minutes

- Total Time: 10-12 minutes

Yield:

- 1 serving

Nutritional Value:

- Calories: 230

- Carbohydrates: 3g

- Protein: 25g

- Fat: 10g

- Fiber: 0g

- Sugar: 1g

9. Tandoori-Style Baked Fish

Ingredients:

- 1 white fish fillet (e.g., tilapia, cod)

- 1/2 cup plain Greek yogurt

- 1/2 tablespoon tandoori spice mix

- 1/2 lemon, juiced

- Salt and pepper to taste

Procedure:

1. Turn the oven on to 375°F, or 190°C.

2. Combine the tandoori spice mix, lemon juice, salt, and pepper with the plain Greek yogurt in a bowl.

3. Apply the yogurt mixture to the fish fillet.

4. Transfer the fish with coating to a baking dish.

5. Bake for 15 to 20 minutes in a preheated oven, or until the yogurt forms a flavorful crust and the fish is thoroughly cooked.

6. Serve the baked fish in the tandoori style as a fiery, high-protein meal.

Time Frame:

- Preparation Time: 10 minutes

- Baking Time: 15-20 minutes

- Total Time: 25-30 minutes

Yield:

- 1 serving

Nutritional Value:

- Calories: 240

- Carbohydrates: 5g

- Protein: 25g

- Fat: 12g

- Fiber: 2g

- Sugar: 3g

10. Lemon Dill Salmon Patties

Ingredients:

- 1 can (6 oz) pink salmon, drained

- 1/4 cup whole wheat breadcrumbs

- 1/2 lemon, juiced

- Fresh dill, chopped

- 1/2 egg, beaten

- Salt and pepper to taste

Procedure:

1. The drained pink salmon, whole wheat breadcrumbs, lemon juice, fresh dill, beaten egg, salt, and pepper should all be combined in a bowl.

2. Create patties out of the mixture.

3. Cook the salmon patties in a skillet until they are cooked through and have a golden-brown color.

4. Present the savory and omega-3-rich salmon patties with dill.

Time Frame:

- Preparation Time: 10 minutes

- Cooking Time: 10 minutes

- Total Time: 20 minutes

Yield:

- 1 serving

Nutritional Value:

- Calories: 230

- Carbohydrates: 15g

- Protein: 25g

- Fat: 10g

- Fiber: 3g

- Sugar: 3g

Meatless Meals

1. Lentil and Vegetable Stew

Ingredients:

- 1 cup lentils

- 2 cups mixed vegetables (carrots, celery, bell peppers)

- 1/2 onion, diced

- 2 cloves garlic, minced

- 4 cups vegetable broth

- 1/2 tablespoon olive oil

- Salt and pepper to taste

Procedure:

1. Warm up the olive oil in a big pot on medium heat.

2. Diced onion and minced garlic should be sautéed until aromatic.

3. Add the vegetable broth, mixed veggies, and lentils.

4. Add pepper and salt for seasoning.

5. Simmer the lentils and vegetables for 30 to 40 minutes, or until they are soft.

6. Serve the vegetable and lentil stew as a filling, high-fiber meal.

Time Frame:

- Preparation Time: 10 minutes

- Cooking Time: 30-40 minutes

- Total Time: 40-50 minutes

Yield:

- 4 servings

Nutritional Value:

- Calories: 220

- Carbohydrates: 40g

- Protein: 15g

- Fat: 2g

- Fiber: 10g

- Sugar: 5g

2. Chickpea and Spinach Curry

Ingredients:

- 1 can (15 oz) chickpeas, drained and rinsed

- 2 cups fresh spinach

- 1/2 onion, diced

- 2 cloves garlic, minced

- 1/2 can (7 oz) diced tomatoes

- 1/2 tablespoon olive oil

- Curry spices (e.g., cumin, coriander, turmeric)

- Salt and pepper to taste

Procedure:

1. Heat the olive oil in a skillet over medium heat.

2. Diced onion and minced garlic should be sautéed until aromatic.

3. Add the diced tomatoes, fresh spinach, chickpeas, and curry powder.

4. Add pepper and salt for seasoning.

5. Simmer until the spinach is wilted and the chickpeas are thoroughly heated, about 15 to 20 minutes.

6. Serve this tasty, plant-based curry made with chickpeas and spinach.

Time Frame:

- Preparation Time: 10 minutes

- Cooking Time: 15-20 minutes

- Total Time: 25-30 minutes

Yield:

- 2 servings

Nutritional Value:

- Calories: 250

- Carbohydrates: 40g

- Protein: 15g

- Fat: 5g

- Fiber: 10g

- Sugar: 5g

3. Eggplant Parmesan

Ingredients:

- 1 small eggplant, sliced

- 1/2 cup whole wheat breadcrumbs

- 1/2 cup no-sugar-added marinara sauce

- 1/4 cup part-skim mozzarella cheese, grated

- 1/2 tablespoon olive oil

- Salt and pepper to taste

Procedure:

1. Turn the oven on to 375°F, or 190°C.

2. Arrange sliced eggplant, mozzarella cheese, marinara sauce, and whole wheat breadcrumbs in a baking dish.

3. Pour some olive oil on top.

4. Add pepper and salt for seasoning.

5. Bake for about 20 to 25 minutes in a preheated oven, or until the cheese is golden and bubbling and the eggplant is soft.

6. Serve this low-calorie, comforting dish of eggplant parmesan.

Time Frame:

- Preparation Time: 10 minutes

- Baking Time: 20-25 minutes

- Total Time: 30-35 minutes

Yield:

- 2 servings

Nutritional Value:

- Calories: 220

- Carbohydrates: 30g

- Protein: 10g

- Fat: 7g

- Fiber: 10g

- Sugar: 5g

4. Quinoa and Black Bean Chili

Ingredients:

- 1 cup quinoa

- 1 can (15 oz) black beans, drained and rinsed

- 1/2 can (7 oz) diced tomatoes

- 1/2 onion, diced

- 2 cloves garlic, minced

- Chili spices (e.g., chili powder, cumin, paprika)

- Salt and pepper to taste

Procedure:

1. Quinoa, black beans, diced tomatoes, diced onion, minced garlic, and chili spices should all be combined in a big pot.

2. Add pepper and salt for seasoning.

3. When the ingredients are covered with water, add more and bring to a boil.

4. For fifteen to twenty minutes, or until the quinoa is thoroughly cooked, reduce heat and simmer.

5. Serve the black bean and quinoa chili as a high-fiber, high-protein dish.

Time Frame:

- Preparation Time: 10 minutes

- Cooking Time: 15-20 minutes

- Total Time: 25-30 minutes

Yield:

- 4 servings

Nutritional Value:

- Calories: 260

- Carbohydrates: 45g

- Protein: 15g

- Fat: 4g

- Fiber: 10g

- Sugar: 3g

5. Stuffed Bell Peppers with Lentils

Ingredients:

- 2 bell peppers

- 1/2 cup cooked green or brown lentils

- 1/2 can (7 oz) diced tomatoes

- 1/4 cup part-skim mozzarella cheese, grated

- 1/2 onion, diced

- 2 cloves garlic, minced

- Salt and pepper to taste

Procedure:

1. Turn the oven on to 375°F, or 190°C.

2. Slice off the bell peppers' tops, then take out the seeds.

3. Cooked lentils, chopped onion, diced tomatoes, minced garlic, salt, and pepper should all be combined in a bowl.

4. Place the lentil mixture inside the bell peppers and cover with mozzarella cheese.

5. The stuffed bell peppers should be put on a baking dish.

6. Bake for about 20 to 25 minutes, or until the cheese is bubbling and the peppers are soft, in a preheated oven.

7. Serve the protein-rich and gratifying stuffed bell peppers with lentils.

Time Frame:

- Preparation Time: 15 minutes

- Baking Time: 20-25 minutes

- Total Time: 35-40 minutes

Yield:

- 2 servings

Nutritional Value:

- Calories: 250

- Carbohydrates: 45g

- Protein: 15g

- Fat: 4g

- Fiber: 10g

- Sugar: 6g

6. Spinach and Feta Stuffed Mushrooms

Ingredients:

- 8 large mushrooms, cleaned and stems removed

- 1 cup fresh spinach, chopped

- 1/4 cup feta cheese, crumbled

- 2 cloves garlic, minced

- 1/2 tablespoon olive oil

- Salt and pepper to taste

Procedure:

1. Turn the oven on to 375°F, or 190°C.

2. Heat the olive oil in a skillet over medium-high heat.

3. Garlic, minced, and sauté until fragrant.

4. Cook the chopped spinach until it wilts.

5. Put the cooked spinach, feta crumbles, salt, and pepper in a bowl.

6. Fill the caps of each mushroom with the spinach-feta mixture.

7. The stuffed mushrooms should be put in a baking dish.

8. Bake for 15 to 20 minutes, or until the filling is golden and the mushrooms are soft, in a preheated oven.

9. Serve the stuffed mushrooms with spinach and feta as a tasty, low-calorie appetizer.

Time Frame:

- Preparation Time: 10 minutes

- Baking Time: 15-20 minutes

- Total Time: 25-30 minutes

Yield:

- 4 servings

Nutritional Value:

- Calories: 90

- Carbohydrates: 5g

- Protein: 5g

- Fat: 6g

- Fiber: 2g

- Sugar: 2g

7. Butternut Squash and Apple Soup

Ingredients:

- 2 cups butternut squash, peeled and diced

- 2 apples, peeled, cored, and diced

- 1/2 onion, diced

- 2 cloves garlic, minced

- 4 cups vegetable broth

- 1/2 tablespoon olive oil

- Salt and pepper to taste

Procedure:

1. Warm up the olive oil in a big pot on medium heat.

2. Diced onion and minced garlic should be sautéed until aromatic.

3. Incorporate the apples, butternut squash, and vegetable broth.

4. Add pepper and salt for seasoning.

5. Simmer the apples and squash for 20 to 25 minutes, or until they are soft.

6. Puree the soup with an immersion blender until it's smooth.

7. Serve the apple and butternut squash soup as a nourishing and cozy choice.

Time Frame:

- Preparation Time: 10 minutes

- Cooking Time: 20-25 minutes

- Total Time: 30-35 minutes

Yield:

- 4 servings

Nutritional Value:

- Calories: 120

- Carbohydrates: 30g

- Protein: 2g

- Fat: 1g

- Fiber: 6g

- Sugar: 15g

8. Ratatouille

Ingredients:

- 1 eggplant, diced

- 1 zucchini, sliced

- 1 bell pepper, sliced

- 1/2 onion, diced

- 2 cloves garlic, minced

- 1/2 can (7 oz) diced tomatoes

- Fresh herbs (e.g., thyme, rosemary)

- 1/2 tablespoon olive oil

- Salt and pepper to taste

Procedure:

1. Heat the olive oil in a skillet over medium-high heat.

2. Diced onion and minced garlic should be sautéed until aromatic.

3. Add the chopped tomatoes, sliced bell pepper, sliced zucchini, and diced eggplant.

4. Add salt, pepper, and fresh herbs for seasoning.

5. Sauté the veggies until they are soft.

6. Present the ratatouille as a savory and nutrient-dense dish.

Time Frame:

- Preparation Time: 10 minutes

- Cooking Time: 20-25 minutes

- Total Time: 30-35 minutes

Yield:

- 4 servings

Nutritional Value:

- Calories: 80

- Carbohydrates: 18g

- Protein: 3g

- Fat: 1g

- Fiber: 5g

- Sugar: 8g

9. Spinach and Chickpea Casserole

Ingredients:

- 1 can (15 oz) chickpeas, drained and rinsed

- 2 cups fresh spinach

- 1/2 onion, diced

- 2 cloves garlic, minced

- 1/2 cup part-skim mozzarella cheese, grated

- Salt and pepper to taste

Procedure:

1. Turn the oven on to 375°F, or 190°C.

2. Chickpeas, chopped onion, minced garlic, and fresh spinach should all be combined in a baking dish.

3. Add pepper and salt for seasoning.

4. Add mozzarella cheese on top.

5. Bake for 20 to 25 minutes, or until the cheese is bubbling and the casserole is thoroughly heated, in a preheated oven.

6. Present the chickpea and spinach casserole as a high-protein, high-calcium dish.

Time Frame:

- Preparation Time: 10 minutes

- Baking Time: 20-25 minutes

- Total Time: 30-35 minutes

Yield:

- 2 servings

Nutritional Value:

- Calories: 240

- Carbohydrates: 30g

- Protein: 15g

- Fat: 6g

- Fiber: 10g

- Sugar: 6g

10. Cauliflower and Sweet Potato Curry

Ingredients:

- 2 cups cauliflower florets

- 1 cup sweet potato, diced

- 1/2 onion, diced

- 2 cloves garlic, minced

- 1 can (15 oz) chickpeas, drained and rinsed

- Curry spices (e.g., curry powder, turmeric, cumin)

- 1/2 tablespoon olive oil

- Salt and pepper to taste

Procedure:

1. Heat the olive oil in a skillet over medium-high heat.

2. Diced onion and minced garlic should be sautéed until aromatic.

3. Add the curry spices, chickpeas, diced sweet potato, and cauliflower florets.

4. Add pepper and salt for seasoning.

5. Sauté the veggies and chickpeas until they are soft as they fully heat up.

6. Present the curry made with sweet potatoes and cauliflower as a savory and high-fiber dish.

Time Frame:

- Preparation Time: 10 minutes

- Cooking Time: 20-25 minutes

- Total Time: 30-35 minutes

Yield:

- 4 servings

Nutritional Value:

- Calories: 220

- Carbohydrates: 40g

- Protein: 10g

- Fat: 4g

- Fiber: 10g

- Sugar: 8g

Diabetes-Friendly Soups And Stews

1. Chicken and Vegetable Soup

Ingredients:

- 1 boneless, skinless chicken breast

- 2 cups mixed vegetables (carrots, celery, peas)

- 1/2 onion, diced

- 2 cloves garlic, minced

- 4 cups low-sodium chicken broth

- Fresh herbs (e.g., thyme, parsley)

- Salt and pepper to taste

Procedure:

1. Low-sodium chicken broth should be added to a large pot and brought to a boil.

2. Add the skinless, boneless chicken breast, mixed vegetables, minced garlic, and diced onion.

3. Add salt, pepper, and fresh herbs for seasoning.

4. Simmer for 20 to 25 minutes, or until the vegetables are soft and the chicken is cooked through.

5. After removing and shredding the chicken, add it back to the soup.

6. Serve the soup with chicken and vegetables as a hearty, high-protein meal.

Time Frame:

- Preparation Time: 10 minutes

- Cooking Time: 20-25 minutes

- Total Time: 30-35 minutes

Yield:

- 4 servings

Nutritional Value:

- Calories: 180

- Carbohydrates: 15g

- Protein: 20g

- Fat: 4g

- Fiber: 4g

- Sugar: 6g

2. Minestrone Soup

Ingredients:

- 1/2 cup whole wheat pasta, small shapes

- 2 cups mixed vegetables (carrots, celery, zucchini)

- 1/2 onion, diced

- 2 cloves garlic, minced

- 4 cups low-sodium vegetable broth

- 1 can (15 oz) diced tomatoes

- Fresh basil leaves, chopped

- Salt and pepper to taste

Procedure:

1. Low-sodium vegetable broth should be added to a large pot and brought to a boil.

2. Add diced tomatoes, mixed vegetables, minced garlic, diced onion, and whole wheat pasta.

3. Add salt, pepper, and fresh basil leaves for seasoning.

4. Simmer the pasta and vegetables for 15 to 20 minutes, or until they are soft.

5. Serve the minestrone soup as a filling, high-fiber meal.

Time Frame:

- Preparation Time: 10 minutes

- Cooking Time: 15-20 minutes

- Total Time: 25-30 minutes

Yield:

- 4 servings

Nutritional Value:

- Calories: 200

- Carbohydrates: 35g

- Protein: 8g

- Fat: 2g

- Fiber: 7g

- Sugar: 8g

3. Tomato Basil Soup

Ingredients:

- 1 can (15 oz) no-sugar-added tomato sauce

- 1 can (15 oz) diced tomatoes

- 1/2 onion, diced

- 2 cloves garlic, minced

- Fresh basil leaves, chopped

- 4 cups low-sodium vegetable broth

- Salt and pepper to taste

Procedure:

1. Low-sodium vegetable broth should be added to a large pot and brought to a boil.

2. Add diced tomatoes, fresh basil leaves, diced onion, minced garlic, and tomato sauce without added sugar.

3. Add pepper and salt for seasoning.

4. Simmer until the flavors are well blended, 15 to 20 minutes.

5. Serve tomato basil soup as a traditional, high-vitamin dish.

Time Frame:

- Preparation Time: 10 minutes

- Cooking Time: 15-20 minutes

- Total Time: 25-30 minutes

Yield:

- 4 servings

Nutritional Value:

- Calories: 100

- Carbohydrates: 20g

- Protein: 5g

- Fat: 1g

- Fiber: 5g

- Sugar: 10g

4. Lentil and Spinach Stew

Ingredients:

- 1 cup green or brown lentils

- 2 cups fresh spinach

- 1/2 onion, diced

- 2 cloves garlic, minced

- 4 cups low-sodium vegetable broth

- Curry spices (e.g., cumin, coriander, turmeric)

- Salt and pepper to taste

Procedure:

1. Low-sodium vegetable broth should be added to a large pot and brought to a boil.

2. Stir in lentils, curry powder, minced garlic, and chopped onion.

3. Add pepper and salt for seasoning.

4. Simmer until the lentils are soft, 20 to 25 minutes.

5. Add the fresh spinach, stir, and cook until it wilts.

6. Serve the flavorful, high-protein lentil and spinach stew.

Time Frame:

- Preparation Time: 10 minutes

- Cooking Time: 20-25 minutes

- Total Time: 30-35 minutes

Yield:

- 4 servings

Nutritional Value:

- Calories: 200

- Carbohydrates: 35g

- Protein: 15g

- Fat: 2g

- Fiber: 8g

- Sugar: 4g

5. Split Pea and Ham Soup

Ingredients:

- 1 cup split peas

- 1 cup lean ham, diced

- 2 carrots, diced

- 1/2 onion, diced

- 2 cloves garlic, minced

- 4 cups low-sodium vegetable broth

- Fresh thyme leaves

- Salt and pepper to taste

Procedure:

1. Low-sodium vegetable broth should be added to a large pot and brought to a boil.

2. Toss in the split peas, chopped ham, chopped onion, chopped carrots, minced garlic, and fresh thyme leaves.

3. Add pepper and salt for seasoning.

4. Simmer until the split peas are soft and the soup has thickened, about 40 to 50 minutes.

5. Serve the ham and split pea soup as a filling, high-protein meal.

Time Frame:

- Preparation Time: 10 minutes

- Cooking Time: 40-50 minutes

- Total Time: 50-60 minutes

Yield:

- 4 servings

Nutritional Value:

- Calories: 180

- Carbohydrates: 30g

- Protein: 15g

- Fat: 2g

- Fiber: 12g

- Sugar: 4g

6. Spicy Black Bean Soup

Ingredients:

- 2 cans (15 oz each) low-sodium black beans, drained and rinsed

- 1/2 onion, diced

- 2 cloves garlic, minced

- 1 bell pepper, diced

- 1 can (15 oz) diced tomatoes

- 4 cups low-sodium vegetable broth

- Chili spices (e.g., cayenne, chili powder, paprika)

- Salt and pepper to taste

Procedure:

1. Low-sodium vegetable broth should be added to a large pot and brought to a boil.

2. Add the diced tomatoes, diced onion, minced garlic, diced bell pepper, drained black beans, and chili powder.

3. Add pepper and salt for seasoning.

4. Let it simmer for 15 to 20 minutes so that the flavors can combine.

5. Serve the fiery black bean soup as a flavorful, high-protein meal.

Time Frame:

- Preparation Time: 10 minutes

- Cooking Time: 15-20 minutes

- Total Time: 25-30 minutes

Yield:

- 4 servings

Nutritional Value:

- Calories: 200

- Carbohydrates: 35g

- Protein: 12g

- Fat: 1g

- Fiber: 10g

- Sugar: 6g

7. Chicken and Barley Soup

Ingredients:

- 1 boneless, skinless chicken breast

- 1/2 cup pearl barley

- 2 carrots, diced

- 2 celery stalks, diced

- 1/2 onion, diced

- 2 cloves garlic, minced

- 4 cups low-sodium chicken broth

- Fresh thyme leaves

- Salt and pepper to taste

Procedure:

1. Low-sodium chicken broth should be added to a large pot and brought to a boil.

2. Add the pearl barley, diced carrots, diced celery, diced onion, minced garlic, and fresh thyme leaves to the boneless, skinless chicken breast.

3. Add pepper and salt for seasoning.

4. Simmer for 30 to 35 minutes, or until the barley is soft and the chicken is cooked through.

5. After removing and shredding the chicken, add it back to the soup.

6. Serve the soup with chicken and barley as a filling, high-fiber meal.

Time Frame:

- Preparation Time: 10 minutes

- Cooking Time: 30-35 minutes

- Total Time: 40-45 minutes

Yield:

- 4 servings

Nutritional Value:

- Calories: 220

- Carbohydrates: 35g

- Protein: 15g

- Fat: 2g

- Fiber: 7g

- Sugar: 4g

8. Beef and Vegetable Stew

Ingredients:

- 1/2 pound lean beef, cubed

- 2 potatoes, diced

- 2 carrots, diced

- 2 celery stalks, diced

- 1/2 onion, diced

- 2 cloves garlic, minced

- 4 cups low-sodium beef broth

- Fresh rosemary leaves

- Salt and pepper to taste

Procedure:

1. Low-sodium beef broth should be added to a large pot and brought to a boil.

2. Add the diced potatoes, carrots, celery, onion, minced garlic, diced beef that has been cubed, and fresh rosemary leaves.

3. Add pepper and salt for seasoning.

4. Simmer until the vegetables are cooked and the beef is tender, about 30 to 35 minutes.

5. Serve the protein-rich and flavorful stew made with beef and vegetables.

Time Frame:

- Preparation Time: 10 minutes

- Cooking Time: 30-35 minutes

- Total Time: 40-45 minutes

Yield:

- 4 servings

Nutritional Value:

- Calories: 240

- Carbohydrates: 30g

- Protein: 20g

- Fat: 4g

- Fiber: 5g

- Sugar: 4g

9. Butternut Squash and Carrot Soup

Ingredients:

- 2 cups butternut squash, diced

- 2 cups carrots, diced

- 1/2 onion, diced

- 2 cloves garlic, minced

- 4 cups low-sodium vegetable broth

- Fresh ginger, grated

- Salt and pepper to taste

Procedure:

1. Low-sodium vegetable broth should be added to a large pot and brought to a boil.

2. Add the minced garlic, grated fresh ginger, diced onion, diced carrots, and diced butternut squash.

3. Add pepper and salt for seasoning.

4. Simmer until the vegetables are soft, 20 to 25 minutes.

5. Puree the soup with an immersion blender until it's smooth.

6. Serve this comforting, high-vitamin soup of butternut squash and carrots.

Time Frame:

- Preparation Time: 10 minutes

- Cooking Time: 20-25 minutes

- Total Time: 30-35 minutes

Yield:

- 4 servings

Nutritional Value:

- Calories: 160

- Carbohydrates: 35g

- Protein: 4g

- Fat: 1g

- Fiber: 6g

- Sugar: 8g

10. Quinoa and Kale Soup

Ingredients:

- 1 cup quinoa, rinsed

- 2 cups fresh kale, chopped

- 1/2 onion, diced

- 2 cloves garlic, minced

- 4 cups low-sodium vegetable broth

- Fresh thyme leaves

- Salt and pepper to taste

Procedure:

1. Low-sodium vegetable broth should be added to a large pot and brought to a boil.

2. Add the rinsed quinoa, chopped fresh kale, minced garlic, diced onion, and fresh thyme leaves.

3. Add pepper and salt for seasoning.

4. Simmer until the quinoa is cooked and the kale has wilted, about 15 to 20 minutes.

5. Serve the kale and quinoa soup as a filling, nutrient-dense dish.

Time Frame:

- Preparation Time: 10 minutes

- Cooking Time: 15-20 minutes

- Total Time: 25-30 minutes

Yield:

- 4 servings

Nutritional Value:

- Calories: 200

- Carbohydrates: 35g

- Protein: 8g

- Fat: 2g

- Fiber: 5g

- Sugar: 4g

Delicious Desserts With Diabetes In Mind

1. Sugar-Free Berry Compote

Ingredients:

- 2 cups mixed berries (strawberries, blueberries, raspberries)

- 1/4 cup water

- 1-2 tablespoons no-calorie sweetener

- 1/2 teaspoon lemon zest

Procedure:

1. Put water, no-calorie sweetener, and mixed berries into a saucepan.

2. Over low heat, bring the mixture to a simmer, stirring from time to time.

3. Simmer for ten to fifteen minutes, or until the mixture thickens and the berries are tender.

4. To add flavor, stir in lemon zest.

5. Before serving, let the sugar-free berry compote cool.

Time Frame:

- Preparation Time: 5 minutes

- Cooking Time: 10-15 minutes

- Total Time: 15-20 minutes

Yield:

- Approximately 4 servings

Nutritional Value:

- Calories: 30

- Carbohydrates: 8g

- Protein: 1g

- Fat: 0g

- Fiber: 3g

- Sugar: 4g

2. Dark Chocolate Avocado Mousse

Ingredients:

- 2 ripe avocados

- 1/4 cup dark cocoa powder

- 1/4 cup no-calorie sweetener

- 1 teaspoon vanilla extract

Procedure:

1. Put ripe avocados, dark cocoa powder, sugar substitute, and vanilla extract in a blender.

2. Blend the mixture until it's creamy and smooth.

3. Before serving, let the food cool in the fridge for at least one hour.

4. Present the avocado mousse with dark chocolate as a decadent yet guilt-free dessert.

Time Frame:

- Preparation Time: 10 minutes

- Chilling Time: 1 hour

- Total Time: 1 hour 10 minutes

Yield:

- Approximately 4 servings

Nutritional Value:

- Calories: 160

- Carbohydrates: 12g

- Protein: 3g

- Fat: 13g

- Fiber: 7g

- Sugar: 1g

3. Baked Cinnamon Apples

Ingredients:

- 4 apples, cored and sliced

- 1 teaspoon ground cinnamon

- 1/4 teaspoon nutmeg

- 1 tablespoon no-calorie sweetener

- 1/4 cup water

- 1/4 cup chopped walnuts (optional)

Procedure:

1. Set the oven's temperature to 175°C/350°F.

2. Put the apple slices, water, nutmeg, ground cinnamon, and sugar substitute in a baking dish.

3. Toss to distribute the spice throughout the apples.

4. Bake the apples for 20 to 25 minutes, or until they are soft.

5. If desired, top with chopped walnuts right before serving.

6. As a cozy, warm treat, serve the baked cinnamon apples.

Time Frame:

- Preparation Time: 10 minutes

- Baking Time: 20-25 minutes

- Total Time: 30-35 minutes

Yield:

- Approximately 4 servings

Nutritional Value:

- Calories: 120

- Carbohydrates: 30g

- Protein: 1g

- Fat: 1g

- Fiber: 5g

- Sugar: 22g

4. Greek Yogurt Parfait with Berries

Ingredients:

- 2 cups non-fat Greek yogurt

- 1 cup mixed berries (strawberries, blueberries, raspberries)

- 2 tablespoons no-calorie sweetener

- 1/4 cup granola (choose a low-sugar variety)

Procedure:

1. Arrange mixed berries, nonfat Greek yogurt, and sugar substitute in serving bowls or glasses.

2. Continue layering as you like.

3. Add granola on top for more texture and crunch.

4. Present the Greek yogurt parfait alongside berries for a tasty and high protein treat.

Time Frame:

- Preparation Time: 5 minutes

- Total Time: 5 minutes

Yield:

- Approximately 2 servings

Nutritional Value:

- Calories: 220

- Carbohydrates: 30g

- Protein: 20g

- Fat: 3g

- Fiber: 5g

- Sugar: 14g

5. Pumpkin Chia Seed Pudding

Ingredients:

- 1/4 cup pumpkin puree

- 2 tablespoons chia seeds

- 1/2 cup unsweetened almond milk

- 1/2 teaspoon pumpkin spice

- 1-2 tablespoons no-calorie sweetener

Procedure:

1. Combine the pureed pumpkin, chia seeds, unsweetened almond milk, pumpkin spice, and sugar substitute in a bowl.

2. Give the ingredients a good stir to fully combine them.

3. To give the chia seeds time to thicken, refrigerate for at least four hours or overnight.

4. Present the creamy and high-fiber pumpkin chia seed pudding as a dessert.

Time Frame:

- Preparation Time: 5 minutes

- Chilling Time: 4 hours or overnight

- Total Time: 4 hours 5 minutes or more

Yield:

- Approximately 2 servings

Nutritional Value:

- Calories: 100

- Carbohydrates: 15g

- Protein: 4g

- Fat: 4g

- Fiber: 9g

- Sugar: 2g

6. Caramelized Banana Slices

Ingredients:

- 2 ripe bananas, sliced

- 1/4 teaspoon ground cinnamon

- 1/4 teaspoon vanilla extract

- 1-2 tablespoons no-calorie sweetener

- Cooking spray or oil for pan

Procedure:

1. Spray cooking spray or oil very lightly in a nonstick pan.

2. Put the pan over medium heat with the banana slices in it.

3. Drizzle the bananas with vanilla extract and ground cinnamon.

4. Cook until the bananas caramelize, 2 to 3 minutes on each side.

5. If you'd like more sweetness, add a dash of sugar substitute.

6. Present the warm, naturally sweet, caramelized banana slices as dessert.

Time Frame:

- Preparation Time: 5 minutes

- Cooking Time: 5-10 minutes

- Total Time: 10-15 minutes

Yield:

- Approximately 2 servings

Nutritional Value:

- Calories: 80

- Carbohydrates: 20g

- Protein: 1g

- Fat: 0g

- Fiber: 3g

- Sugar: 12g

7. No-Sugar-Added Apple Crisp

Ingredients:

- 4 apples, peeled, cored, and sliced

- 1 teaspoon ground cinnamon

- 1/4 teaspoon nutmeg

- 1/2 cup old-fashioned oats

- 1/4 cup almond flour

- 2 tablespoons unsalted butter (or coconut oil for a dairy-free option)

Procedure:

1. Set the oven's temperature to 175°C/350°F.

2. Put the sliced apples, nutmeg, and ground cinnamon in a baking dish.

3. Combine melted unsalted butter (or coconut oil), almond flour, and old-fashioned oats in a different bowl.

4. Cover the apples with the oat mixture.

5. Bake for 30 to 35 minutes, until the apples are soft and the topping is golden.

6. Present the apple crisp with no added sugar as a warm, filling dessert.

Time Frame:

- Preparation Time: 15 minutes

- Baking Time: 30-35 minutes

- Total Time: 45-50 minutes

Yield:

- Approximately 4 servings

Nutritional Value:

- Calories: 180

- Carbohydrates: 30g

- Protein: 3g

- Fat: 7g

- Fiber: 6g

- Sugar: 15g

8. Lemon Berry Sorbet

Ingredients:

- 2 cups mixed berries (strawberries, blueberries, raspberries)

- 1/4 cup no-calorie sweetener

- 2 tablespoons fresh lemon juice

- 1/4 cup water

Procedure:

1. Put water, fresh lemon juice, no-calorie sweetener, and mixed berries into a blender.

2. Process the mixture until it's smooth.

3. Transfer the mixture into an ice cream maker or shallow dish.

4. Freeze the sorbet until it solidifies, about 3–4 hours.

5. As a cool and guilt-free dessert, serve the lemon-berry sorbet.

Time Frame:

- Preparation Time: 10 minutes

- Freezing Time: 3-4 hours

- Total Time: 3 hours 10 minutes or more

Yield:

- Approximately 4 servings

Nutritional Value:

- Calories: 60

- Carbohydrates: 15g

- Protein: 1g

- Fat: 0g

- Fiber: 3g

- Sugar: 9g

9. Sugar-Free Chocolate Pudding

Ingredients:

- 2 cups unsweetened almond milk

- 1/4 cup unsweetened cocoa powder

- 1/4 cup cornstarch

- 1/4 cup no-calorie sweetener

- 1/2 teaspoon vanilla extract

Procedure:

1. Combine cornstarch, no-calorie sweetener, unsweetened almond milk, and unsweetened cocoa powder in a saucepan.

2. Cook, stirring constantly, over medium heat until mixture thickens.

3. Turn off the heat source and mix in the vanilla extract.

4. Fill serving cups with sugar-free chocolate pudding.

5. Before serving, let the food cool in the fridge for at least two hours.

6. Present the low-sugar chocolate pudding as a rich and velvety treat.

Time Frame:

- Preparation Time: 5 minutes

- Chilling Time: 2 hours

- Total Time: 2 hours 5 minutes or more

Yield:

- Approximately 4 servings

Nutritional Value:

- Calories: 40

- Carbohydrates: 9g

- Protein: 2g

- Fat: 2g

- Fiber: 2g

- Sugar: 1g

10. Almond and Coconut Bites

Ingredients:

- 1/2 cup almond butter

- 1/4 cup unsweetened shredded coconut

- 1/4 cup almond flour

- 2 tablespoons no-calorie sweetener

- 1/4 teaspoon vanilla extract

Procedure:

1. Combine almond flour, vanilla extract, unsweetened shredded coconut, almond butter, and calorie-free sweetener in a bowl.

2. Continue mixing until a dough is formed.

3. Using your fingers, roll the dough into bite-sized balls, then transfer them to a baking sheet.

4. To firm up, refrigerate for a minimum of 30 minutes.

5. Present the coconut and almond nibbles as a filling and nutty dessert.

Time Frame:

- Preparation Time: 10 minutes

- Chilling Time: 30 minutes

- Total Time: 40 minutes

Yield:

- Approximately 10-12 bites

Nutritional Value:

- Calories: 100

- Carbohydrates: 4g

- Protein: 3g

- Fat: 8g

- Fiber: 2g

- Sugar: 1g

14-day meal plan

Day 1:

Breakfast:

- Overnight Oatmeal with Berries

- Greek Yogurt Parfait with Berries

Lunch:

- Chicken and Vegetable Stir-Fry

- Steamed Broccoli with Almonds

Dinner:

- Garlic Herb Grilled Shrimp

- Lemon Berry Sorbet

Day 2:

Breakfast:

- Veggie and Cheese Omelette

Lunch:

- Turkey and Spinach Stuffed Peppers

- Roasted Garlic Asparagus

Dinner:

- Spiced Pulled Pork

- Cabbage and Carrot Coleslaw

Day 3:

Breakfast:

- Cinnamon Apple Porridge

Lunch:

- Lemon Herb Grilled Fish

- Lemon Herb Quinoa

Dinner:

- Beef and Bell Pepper Stir-Fry

- Cauliflower Rice with Shrimp

Day 4:

Breakfast:

- Quinoa Breakfast Bowl

Lunch:

- Zucchini Noodles with Pesto and Cherry Tomatoes

- Caprese Skewers

Dinner:

- Balsamic Glazed Chicken

- Ratatouille

Day 5:

Breakfast:

- Scrambled Eggs with Spinach and Tomatoes

Lunch:

- Quinoa and Black Bean Salad

- Green Beans with Garlic and Lemon

Dinner:

- Beef and Mushroom Skillet

- Butternut Squash and Carrot Soup

Day 6:

Breakfast:

- Breakfast Frittata with Turkey Sausage

Lunch:

- Lemon Garlic Roasted Turkey

- Mashed Cauliflower

Dinner:

- Pork and Cabbage Rolls

- Tomato Basil Soup

Day 7:

Breakfast:

- Chia Seed Pudding

Lunch:

- Spinach and Mushroom Stuffed Chicken Breast

- Stuffed Bell Peppers with Quinoa

Dinner:

- Teriyaki Tuna Steaks

- Lemon Dill Salmon Patties

Day 8:

Breakfast:

- Breakfast Burrito with Whole Wheat Tortilla

Lunch:

- Spinach and Feta Stuffed Mushrooms

- Stuffed Bell Peppers with Lentils

Dinner:

- Beef and Vegetable Soup

- Cilantro Lime Brown Rice

Day 9:

Breakfast:

- Baked Avocado and Egg

Lunch:

- Chickpea and Spinach Curry

- Greek Yogurt Dip with Sliced Cucumbers

Dinner:

- Beef and Broccoli Stir-Fry

- Spicy Black Bean Soup

Day 10:

Breakfast:

- Lentil and Vegetable Stew

Lunch:

- Beef and Cabbage Stew

- Baked Brussels Sprouts

Dinner:

- Chicken and Vegetable Curry

- Sugar-Free Berry Compote

Day 11:

Breakfast:

- Dark Chocolate Avocado Mousse

Lunch:

- Lemon Herb Roasted Chicken

- Quinoa and Kale Soup

Dinner:

- Chicken and Asparagus Stir-Fry

- No-Sugar-Added Apple Crisp

Day 12:

Breakfast:

- Pumpkin Chia Seed Pudding

Lunch:

- Pork Tenderloin with Apples
- Ratatouille

Dinner:

- BBQ Turkey Drumsticks
- Caramelized Banana Slices

Day 13:

Breakfast:

- Sugar-Free Chocolate Pudding

Lunch:

- Teriyaki Turkey Tenderloin
- Spinach and Chickpea Casserole

Dinner:

- Lemon Garlic Chicken Breast
- Baked Cinnamon Apple

Day 14:

Breakfast:

- Almond and Coconut Bites

Lunch:

- Coconut-Crusted Cod
- Tomato Basil Soup

Dinner:

- Garlic Butter Scallops
- Quinoa and Black Bean Chili

Conclusion

"The Type 2 Diabetes Crockpot Cookbook" provides a thorough manual for people with Type 2 diabetes as well as their families. This cookbook offers a variety of delectable and diabetes-friendly recipes along with insightful commentary and helpful advice for improved diet-based diabetes management. Let's review the main ideas covered in the cookbook:

1. Understanding Type 2 Diabetes:

- The cookbook begins with a clear explanation of Type 2 diabetes, increasing the reader's awareness of this condition.

- It highlights the crucial role that diet plays in managing diabetes and the impact it has on blood sugar control.

- It emphasizes the unique role that crockpot cooking can play in simplifying and improving the dietary choices of those with Type 2 diabetes.

2. Benefits of Crockpot Cooking for Type 2 Diabetes:

- Slow cooking is presented as a method that can help individuals maintain controlled blood sugar levels.

- The cookbook highlights the benefits of portion control and nutritional balance, making it easier to manage diabetes through meal planning.

- It underlines the convenience and practicality of crockpot cooking, allowing individuals and families to enjoy diabetes-friendly meals without extensive cooking efforts.

3. Benefits of the Book:

- The cookbook is a valuable resource for those looking for diabetes-friendly recipes that cater to their specific dietary needs.

- Nutritional information is provided for each recipe, empowering individuals to make informed choices based on their nutritional requirements.

- The cookbook is designed to suit both individuals and families who are navigating the challenges of managing Type 2 diabetes.

4. Tips and Guidelines for Cooking with Type 2 Diabetes:

- The cookbook offers practical tips for choosing diabetes-friendly ingredients that help control blood sugar levels.

- It encourages readers to monitor their carbohydrate and sugar intake, helping them make conscious dietary choices.

- The cookbook provides guidance on how to balance meals for better blood sugar control, promoting overall health and well-being.

In a world where dietary decisions can have a big influence on health, "The Type 2 Diabetes Crockpot Cookbook" is a great tool for people with Type 2 diabetes and their families. This cookbook offers a route to tasty and health-conscious meals that improve blood sugar control and quality of life with its variety of diabetes-friendly recipes, nutritional data, and helpful advice.

People with Type 2 diabetes can manage their condition and make informed decisions, eat satisfying meals, and improve their health by using the recipes and advice in this cookbook. To ensure that dietary choices are in line with specific health needs, always seek the advice of a registered dietitian or other healthcare professional.

More Titles from The Author Are

1. Super Tasty Air Fryer Cookbook For Beginners
2. Forever Strong Cookbook
3. Super Easy Healthy Cookbook For Beginners
4. The Ultimate Crockpot Cookbook For Beginners
5. The Complete Pressure Pot Cookbook
6. The Ultimate 5 Ingredient Crockpot Cookbook
7. The Complete Crockpot Desserts Cookbook
8. The Ultimate Slow Cooker Cookbook For Beginners
9. The Essential Crockpot Cookbook For Two
10. The Complete Crockpot Soup Cookbook
11. The Ultimate Instant Pot Cookbook For Beginners and lot more

Printed in Great Britain
by Amazon

33048035R00073